How to Get, Build & Keep Your Clientele

What your clients wish you knew.
A Guide Booklet for the Beauty
Service Professional

Mary Carver-Goldring; Stella Carver

WestBow·
PRESS
A DIVISION OF THOMAS NELSON
& ZONDERVAN

WestBow Press books may be ordered through booksellers or by contacting:

WestBow Press
A Division of Thomas Nelson & Zondervan
1663 Liberty Drive
Bloomington, IN 47403
www.westbowpress.com
1 (866) 928-1240

ISBN: 978-1-4908-6834-9 (sc)
ISBN: 978-1-4908-6835-6 (hc)
ISBN: 978-1-4908-6833-2 (e)

Library of Congress Control Number: 2015901584

Print information available on the last page.

WestBow Press rev. date: 6/10/2015

Contents

Dedication Page

From the ♥ of Mary Carver-Goldring
This book is dedicated to my cosmetology teacher
The late Madam Lucille Eddings
and all my classmates at
Eddings Beauty School in Jackson Tennessee
Also to all my Family Affair staff and booth renters.

In loving memory of the following who are absent from the body
in the presence of the Lord
My husband Mr. John Goldring
My mother Narline Timberlake.
My Grandson Thomas Deal
My mentor & former owner of The Family Affair Style Shop I
Doris Taylor-Proctor.

All my fellow stylist & Clients I've known who have passed on.
My Family Affair Family of Stylists
Mrs. Eleanor Gaines & Olivee Brown-Bey

From the ♥ of Stella Carver
My contribution to this book is dedicated to my
sweet loving mother Ms. Mary Carver-Goldring
"she is truly the sweetest thing that ever combed my hair"
My late father, Mr. Luke Carver. My Godson, CJ
Also to my four siblings Debra Collins, Dr. Belinda Carver-Taylor,
Virgil Carver & Terry Carver.
Relatives, sorority sisters and friends who are always supportive and
encouraging of any endeavor that I decide excitingly to undertake.

Gift Purchase

Your opportunity to finally let your Beauty Service Professional know your thoughts.

I, _____ purchased this Guide Booklet for
(Name or Anonymous)

_____, who is/was my _____
(Beauty Service Professional's Name)   (Beauty Service Profession)

Check all that apply:

- o   I want you to know the reason I fired you as my Beauty Service Professional.
- o   I want you to know why I continue to patronize your service.
- o   I want you to know, I think your Beauty Service Establishment needs to make some improvements.
- o   I want you to know, I wish you were more motivated to improve overall.
- o   I want you to know, I wish you would improve your skill level so I will get my money's worth.
- o   I want you to know, I really like you as a person, but you need to be more professional.
- o   I want you to know, _____
  _____
  _____

Personal Note (What I wish you knew):

_____
_____
_____
_____

Paying the Price for $uccess

Are You <u>WILLING</u> To Give Yourself A Successful Future???

You are holding in your hand and reading one of the best Motivational Information Tools you could have ever decided to pick up. It's a tool, a key that opens a locked door; it's like a hammer to your nail. If you've been sleepwalking … Wake up! The Beauty Service Profession is a dynamic industry. You can personally determine **by your work ethic** how much money you want to make and how much time you want to spend making it. YOU will meet great people and then YOU will help them establish and maintain their personal image, relieve their stress, help them help the world be a better place. WOW, look at you! With this first page, **ready set, get started** to apply Wisdom and Tips gathered from your author a BSP-*Beauty Service Professional* who's made a successful career and wants to share the knowledge gained with you.

◀))) Think About This …

Building and Keeping a strong Clientele is like a (GWP) *Guaranteed Weekly Paycheck!*

With base Clients scheduled regularly each week, you can determine how much you will make and plan your financial life accordingly. Building and keeping your clientele is a skill that can be learned. Take 30 minutes out of your day to read and internalized the following easy principles outlined in this Guide Booklet. Once you begin to apply the skills learned and techniques you'll be on your way to realizing any goal you set for yourself in the wonderful Beauty Service Industry of Cosmetology, Barbering, Nail Tech, Esthetician, Massage therapy etc.

Are you willing to pay the price for success? "If you are not willing to pay the price for success, you are setting yourself up to pay the price for failure!"

🔊 **Think Abut This** …

How many salons do your clients pass to get to yours? 2, 5, 7, 9 Guess? Then count them from your front door to the salon on the next trip there. Then, simply decide to be better than your competition.

Building New Clients

A new client that sits in your chair for the first time has the potential to bring you $1,540 per year. (That is a very conservative estimate) Over the course of your career that could be thousands of dollars depending on how many clients you have. For example: 1 Client coming every two weeks for regular service at $50.00 (18 weeks x $50= $900) and getting a special service every six weeks at $80.00 (8 weeks x $80 =$640) *Based on 52 weeks in a year, this is a very conservative estimate. If you are a nail tech, barber etc. figure out the average cost of service and design the above example specific to your profession. Begin to think like a BSP not a person enjoying their favorite hobby.

Keeping Existing Clients

Based on the above example a client that has been coming to you for 5 years is worth $7700. If you ask the opinion of a woman or man, they will tell you that finding a *good* Beauty Service Professional

BSP- is like finding a good doctor. Once you find one, you want to keep he or she for life and you will not hesitate to tell your family, friends, co-workers, church members etc. about your great discovery!

Soooooo ... **Ready, Set, Go!**

Frequently Used Acronyms in this guide booklet.

- BSE–Beauty Service Establishment
- BSI–Beauty Service Industry
- BSP–Beauty Service Professional
- CIS–Client Information Sheet
- GWP–Guaranteed Weekly Paycheck
- UBSP–Unprofessional Beauty Service Person.

Suggestions ... How to Effectively Use This Guide Book

This guide booklet is designed to be simple and easy to use. Give yourself a motivational week to read it and complete the worksheets and questionnaires. Flip through the pages first to familiarize yourself with the contents. Hopefully you've read page 1, "Are you willing to pay the price for success," if so you've got the question. Now read on for the answers. Keep **read**ing and **think**ing and making your game plan. Use the note space at the end of each chapter to **brainstorm** and **record** your first thoughts and reactions to the information. **Feel** and **hear** that positive self talk in your head as you get re-energized to make this profession work for you. Add, create & explore new affirmations that work to get you back on the right successful track.

Once you're familiar with the contents go on and complete the "**Before**" Self Evaluation on page 49. Once you've <u>finished the entire guide booklet</u> you can complete the "**After**" Self Evaluation and hopefully your answers *after* you finish are much better than the *before* answers. You need to be extremely and deliberately honest with yourself as you evaluate yourself. So take a deep breath raise that pencil and get ready to circle yes or no **honestly**. Choose to keep the booklet at home or in a safe location so you can do the evaluation in privacy and remember to cut yourself some slack while in that self reflection mode. Remember today is the first day of the rest of your life, tomorrow is a new day to make some changes and give yourself the gift of success.

Another way to evaluate and correct *you*, (me, myself and I) the fully capable person; is to have an **AP**-*Accountability Partner*. Choose wisely an AP that is also committed to making improvements in some way. This can be a co-worker, friend or family member. They too should be on a "making improvement" journey so they can relate when you start succeeding and feeling great about yourself. It helps your AP not be so brutally critical because you'll both be feeling the emotional ride that comes with changing for the better, breaking out of a rut! *Because*, it will be an emotional ride. The AP can be more supportive and encouraging to you if they are on a similar or the same journey. It's so important that you chose carefully so this person will not become a discouragement to the process of progress! You can both help keep each other motivated and accountable in the best way you agree upon. Perhaps you can really get dressed up and go out and celebrate in style by making a dinner reservation at your favorite expensive restaurant each quarter. Here are some other possible goals or milestones you can shoot for with your AP: Opening that IRA-Retirement account or saving $500 emergency cash or getting to work thirty minutes to an hour early each day for a month. You'll discover some more ideas as you read along, especially after you complete the self-evaluations.

As you are well aware, this BSI–Beauty Service Industry is a career you should feel grateful and blessed to be apart of. Armed with your skill set and professional license you are off to the races in one of the most exciting careers ever. It offers the most flexible hours. Plus, you can have the most fun and be rewarded handsomely if you are continually learning and getting excited about these possibilities that your effort and attitude turn into reality. And it's an international industry; everyone wants and needs our service all around the world. Self motivation, goal setting and improving your skills and tools for success are the key that unlock our potential to maximizing our longevity and reaching all of our financial, personal and professional goals. I say "our" because we should all strive to continue learning and growing as trends change and new social media tools are invented etc. etc. The world is ever evolving and changing why shouldn't WE?

So read on and please write or email us with questions and comments about the guide booklet as well. Fill our cup to overflowing with your thoughts on how to improve it or what you'd like to see included in the future. Visit the website to order more tools for success and like us on Facebook to hear what others are saying about their success and add your comments.

The 10 Basic Key Points to Keeping and building a Healthy "full to overflowing" Clientele

The 10 Basic Key Points to Keeping and Building a Healthy Clientele

The 10 Keys

1. You must begin each day with Positive Prayer, Affirmations, Focus and Faith.
2. Never underestimate the importance of a Good First Impression.
3. Always complete a full and thorough consultation on the client's first visit.
4. Have a consultation, information talk when giving a client any new service.
5. Always be professional, even with relatives, friends and long time clients.
6. Do unto others as you would have them do unto you.
7. Always respect your client's time.
8. Be sure your Sterilization and Sanitation practices are up to date.
9. Keep your trade supplies, marketing tools, client rewards plentiful.
10. Always do your very best, no matter who the client is.

As you read the 10 Keys above I'm sure you completed a mental checklist of what you are doing, what you may not be doing and areas that need improvement. The keys sound simple right? You may even be saying to yourself, I always do number 1 and number 8. Read them again now and remember, the most important person to be honest with is always the person staring at you in your own mirror. I'm sure you *know'em* well in all their glory, that priceless and precious person behind your very own eyeballs. So please be honest as you read the Keys again and reflect on each one key point at a time. The honest question to ask yourself as you look at each Key is, "Is this Key something I practice consistently?" Also be honest that the truth is, these 10 key points really are simple once they become habits. They should be a consistent true way of professional life. If you aren't already, you can do it starting today. You should do it! Why wouldn't you do it?

If you knew a better, more efficient or quicker way to be more successful would you be willing to change for the better? Think about the brain under your hair and remember that you can change your mind and guess what? Your actions will follow. You can plan to improve your thinking and skill set as the world changes. Just as new technology becomes available, the economy and needs of the community do change. We are human's we can learn, change and adapt. To keep on improving, growing and learning and deciding to be better are always goals worth reaching. But some things remain constant and the ten keys are the basic rules of getting new clients and keeping the ones you have. The basics like good old fashioned customer service, believing in yourself and each day repeating your good habits, again and again and again will keep your Appointment Book full of clients to service.

There are many goals to achieve in this guide booklet. It has been designed to give you the skills, ideas and tools to ease the fear of loosing clients or sitting all day with no one to service or having to work a part-time job to supplement doing what you love to do.

Read on and get ready to plant seeds of success so that you will reap a harvest of clients. If you *apply* these 10 key points you will most definitely be unable to service all the clients because there will be so many. Remember clients can get your service at a number of convenient locations around town. Why do or didn't they choose you in the first place and why do or didn't they keep coming back to you? You will know the answer to these questions and have a whole lot more to say about that when you turn the last page of this guide booklet. So open your heart and get ready to examine with kindness your professional behavior, honestly reading and applying the tools and techniques written just for you.

Another question for you: Just think about your cell phone? How many upgrades have you had since your very first one? Well, when is the last time you've upgraded your thinking? Do you have a two year contract with yourself to re-evaluate your PLAN for the future? Are you accountable to you for saving and paying yourself first, what about keeping up-to-date on current trends, your marketing tools, reaching out to new clients, thanking the existing clients? I hope you answered yes to all those questions. If you answered yes, you are a BSP. But if you answered no, then you may be a BSH-Beauty Service Hobbyist. Your business is a hobby that you don't take too seriously.

I can't wait to grow up! Uh, remember saying that as a frustrated child. Well here we are, all grown up. Now we know that adult life is a series of making decisions, choices and benefiting or suffering from the consequences of those choices. As a child we want that freedom so desperately. We don't want our parents, guardians, teachers, older siblings and adults telling us what to do. Unfortunately we don't realize that growing up is a process and hopefully as we grow in years we've learned some good habits. If not, we will pay the price for bad habits along the way. "Youth is wasted on the young" and "If I knew then what I know now" comes to mind. But just know this for sure, "it's never too late to get an early start on future success." You can quote the booklet on that one.

The 10 keys are not in order of importance because each one is individually and collectively important. They are habits that when you master them you will be on the road to building and keeping a good satisfied clientele.

If you find yourself reading this guide booklet today because your business is failing, or you find yourself deeply in debt, perhaps your clients are avoiding eye contact, you feel embarrassed of the condition of your place of work, then stop and get excited. Today is the first day of the rest of your life and it's getting ready to change for the better because you've decided it should.

Thoughts/Ideas: _____

_____

_____

_____

_____

_____

_____

_____

_____

_____

_____

_____

_____

_____

_____

_____

_____

_____

The detailed overview of the 10 Key Points to Keeping and Building a Healthy Clientele.

1. YOUR DAY & OUTLOOK MUST BEGIN WITH PRAYER, AFFIRMATIONS, FOCUS & FAITH.

Because … In order to give yourself the gift of success, you must first believe you deserve it. Your life, the outlook for your day must begin with you feeling positive and seeking what you desire. So, practice waking up and immediately focusing your mind on a positive affirmation such as: "this is gonna be an awesome day," "this is gonna be a $500 day," "with God nothing will be impossible for my success today." You must believe that you can achieve your goals **if** you knew how. Don't let your mind be idle and wake up with a, "Lord what mishap or craziness will I face today." It's as if you feel you have no control and you're willing to accept what comes.

Ms. Mary Personal Experience: *For many years I've practiced this habit: Every morning when I wake up, I immediately give thanks to God for my health, strength, family, friends and my clients who are like my family and many are my true friends. After that I read the daily word and meditate on the scripture and message. My daily prayer is "may I be a blessing to someone, just as I am blessed." Many people have asked me over the years how I stay so positive and happy? I attribute it to the way I start my day. This positive start to my day has strengthened me for the times I had to endure sadness and loss as well as opened me to fully enjoy all my blessings each day. Our clients over the years have been through many wonderful experiences, they've endured hardships, joys and tragic sadness. I always try to have an encouraging word and a shoulder for the time that they are in my presence. I genuinely respect, love and care about my clients and I guess it shows. I've had a steady clientele and many of my clients have been with me for 20 to 30 + years or more. Some leave and when they find their way back, they are more grateful the second time around.*

A great and life changing habit to begin is to start your day wanting success, you've got to ask, seek and find success. Success is not some mysterious gift given to a few lucky people. It's for anyone who asks, develops the skill, talent and good habits to grab hold of it. Success is for anyone who will choose to **focus** their attention and efforts on achieving it. You must desire it for yourself by bravely and courageously saying *positive* affirmations such as, "I will be successful in my business." "I will work smarter, not just harder." **Affirmations** are positive words and phrases that affirm our desired outcome. However you want your life to be … you must see it that way first. Dream it.

If you're struggling financially in this lucrative career, you could unknowingly be saying negative affirmations to yourself otherwise known as negative self-talk. If you say things to yourself like, "I don't have any clients, they just disappeared and stopped coming"! Maybe you've never honestly chosen to ask yourself why they stopped coming. You've never asked yourself or made **you** accountable for any failure you may be experiencing. What you may be afraid to face is that "what ever the reason you have no clients is … you are surely suffering the consequences of their choice not to patronize your business. The choice to never ask why or find solutions to your problems is not the mindset of a successful BSP. Trust and believe there are always solutions to every problem.

Sometimes we don't ask because we are not prepared to fix what is broken. Recognize if this is you; Are you currently riding and quiet comfortably seated on the self-pity, negative self talk train? How long have you been on the pity party train, because it is not a free train ride? It's costing you time, money, peace and joy. Get off that train and get on the positive affirmation super highway in a red convertible Lamborghini headed for your very own personally designed, developed dream future. Zoom-Zoom Baby!

In the past remember a time when you were focused on a positive future? You had a positive and motivated outlook for your life. Something inspired you and you began your collection of self help books, took some classes at a few trade shows, watched or listened to a motivational speaker. However you've read the self help books yet stopped or never applied the information you learned? Or worse you've never read them but keep them prominently displayed to remind yourself you did try back then.

Well this first key, to keep that positive outlook is nothing new, you know that all basic success strategies begin by telling you the basic way to start and end the day when trying to reach your goals is with positive thoughts, clear goals and mustard seed faith in your goals.

Remember … yeah it's coming back to you, that first rule is to write down your dreams and goals. You've got to see yourself successful. Close your eyes and **visualize** how it will look once you achieve goals. Know what it would **feel** like, feel the stress of foolishness and failure leave you as you take checks to the bank or swipe your clients debit cards sending money into your account automatically or better yet using your smart phone to collect your client's payment. These of course are visuals of the self-employed. If you are an employee at a prestigious Day Spa or on commission you can create the visual that will motivate you to make the choice to choose success. Make it a habit every morning and before you go to bed at night to **pray** (which is simply talking, asking, being assured you're being heard) ask and be thankful sincerely for the success of the day and of your future success.

As you drift off to sleep at night remember to actively **focus your mind** and see yourself being successful, handling your business in a professional way with so many satisfied clients, smiling, coming and going. Positively visualize your appointment book being filled with clients and lunch breaks being scheduled, days off clearly marked for your personal obligations. Visualize people calling you and you searching turning pages for a convenient spot to place them in. Scream YES, I am in demand! As you fall asleep repeat, I am in demand, I am in demand, I am in demand zzzzzz.

Have **faith** and confidence that you can achieve this goal and maintain it. You must know your worth and your clients worth to give and do your best always for a successful future in this BSI-Beauty Service Industry. There are so many books and studies being done currently on the results of positive thinking, prayer and focus. It's not a gimmick, positive prayer, focus and faith works; there are scientific studies that prove it. You become what you think about the most. In your head … Instead of choosing worry, fear, and uncertainty start thinking and seeing you, yourself being successful. How are you dressed each day? Do you have on a clean nice smock or a uniform (no ripped pockets, fading lettering, too small or too large fitted work garments)? Is your hair, nails, skin and personal appearance a representation of the service you offer? Look in the mirror, do you look successful, do you look like you care about you? If not, start with an image make-over for yourself.

Another great idea is to go and experience the service you provide somewhere anonymously. See how it feels to get the service you provide. Hopefully you'll have a great experience that you can learn from, but if not you'll see how it feels to be treated as though your time isn't important or that you as a client don't matter.

♂**Quote:** Ms. Dorothy "Dot" Jones, Client for over 40 years

On Wednesday morning I have a standing appointment with a young lady that greets you with a big smile saying "I'm great." She is happy, cheerful and with cape in hand saying, "Come on back." With Loving Hands, she does magic on my hair. Giving words of advice on health and just common every day sense. She is a jewel – the young lady, My Beautician – Mary Goldring

Thoughts/Ideas: _____

_____

_____

_____

_____

_____

_____

_____

_____

_____

_____

_____

_____

_____

_____

_____

_____

_____

_____

_____

_____

_____

2. KNOW & R.E.S.P.E.C.T. THE IMPORTANCE OF A GOOD FIRST IMPRESSION.

Because … A fully trained, professional and informed staff is the best memorable **good first impression** that will give the client an idea of what is in store for them. Together with a clean, modern, organized and well maintained salon this is the *knock out-one two punch* of a client relaxing and trusting that hey, "I may have found MY new place." "Let me tweet or FB this to my friends." A bad first impression can be costly from the client who easily spreads the news of their terrible experience. Let's face it.

A great first impression happens when a new or existing client is greeted by name and a welcoming statement is made. This is extremely important. Always greet your clients by name with a reassuring smile, acknowledging by that quick glance that you see them, you know they are here waiting for service. A quick acknowledging glance can say in an instant that you are glad and thankful to see them. For many it may be the only smile they get that day. Also it's the moment to let them know verbally you'll be with them in a moment or a time to let them know if you are running more than ten or fifteen minutes behind schedule. Communication goes such a long way in easing your clients stress and yours on the day and time of their appointment.

When your newly scheduled clients that aren't familiar to you come in perhaps they've never been to your establishment, you'll recognize that deer in the headlights, "I need help, what do I do" look instantly. It's wonderful if you have trained front desk staff, or an assistant to greet clients. But if not you can stop what you're doing, excuse yourself to meet a new client as soon as they walk in and get them set up with the Client Consultation Card on a clip board with an ink pen or if you're tech savvy give them the Tablet to complete the Client Consultation Card. Be sure to give them a tour of the salon, where the bathrooms and water cooler are. Ask if they have a favorite magazine or want to look at hair style books and give them the most recent edition. What ever courtesy or conveniences you are offering while clients wait or are being serviced take them or point it out to them. From a water cooler, to a snack machine or full restaurant next door, to current magazines, trend books, to a full boutique and retail area make sure your clients know it's all for them.

◀))) Think about this ... Don't be afraid to partner with the businesses around you for a mutually beneficial relationship. Your clients will patronize nearby businesses and you want to take advantage of that. Work out a discount with the restaurant next door for your clients, perhaps giving clients a coupon for use on the day of service or just for new clients only. Don't abuse the privilege and be honest and respectful of the agreement. Ask the business next door to let you advertise on their menu or leave business cards in their waiting area. If there is a clothing store next door, perhaps have postcards made to give to their exiting customers stating, "Top that new outfit off with a hairstyle from the Sassi Beauty Salon." A fitness center nearby your BSE, "After you sweat it off, we can relax it away with a quick muscle relaxing massage"

Make sure your clients can lounge comfortably in a clean, comfortable area and relax for a moment before their service. Have assistants prepared and trained to keep those areas stocked, clean and neat. For a new client the welcoming greeting will go something like: "Good afternoon Ms. Smith we've been expecting you and it's so nice to meet you, I'm Jasmine, Michelle's assistant. Please have a seat right here and take a moment to fill out our Client Consultation Card. Also I want to point out that the restroom is right down this hall to the right and there is a water cooler in the hallway as well. Existing clients should be greeted as well: Good morning Ms. Taylor, Michelle will be with you in fifteen minutes or Michelle is ready for you so follow me. New clients will know they are in the right place and have made a wise decision in choosing your establishment.

A welcoming statement can include an honest complement and should always be positive. Even if the client looks tired and stressed, you could say, Ms. Smith I hope you're having a great day so far or I hope you're looking forward to a positive weekend. Because when you say to a client, "Ms. Smith you look tired and stressed" or "Is everything alright Ms. Smith," if she isn't tired and stressed or everything is alright you've just made a criticism without intending to do so. Positive statements such as, "Isn't the weather beautiful," or we really needed all this rain for the spring flowers to bloom" can be relaxing and put clients in a more positive mood.

First Impressions are crucial to the success of any business. Many potentially new clients will walk right past a salon and decide if the atmosphere is inviting and right for them. Stand outside and peer through your own window. Then take note of people walking by your establishment. Visually put a dollar sign over each head. If the salon, barber shop or spa looks dirty, clients and staff are talking loud, ignoring clients, stylist slouching watching Jerry Springer, eating at their stations, appearing to be gossiping with their clients or each other it could be a turn off and cost you future clients. Ask yourself, how much longer I will watch all those dollar signs walk right past this BSE window. Walk to the door on your break and hand out some business cards, postcards, brochures or flyers. Invite clients to come in. Chat with them about their needs, don't assume they don't need your service.

Imagine this scenario for a moment, new client's walk in and no one acknowledges them quickly or professionally. They stand at the front desk fidgeting and looking for someone, anyone to acknowledge and help them. They may not even schedule an appointment or if they do they may not keep it. That's a huge loss because they are most likely local to the area and your salon may be very convenient for them. It can be a little or a lot intimidating to walk in to a non-professional salon and ask a question. All eyes turn, looking the potential client up and down realizing they are unfamiliar to the salon. Instead of greeting the person with a warm smile and a professional "How can I help you," the potential client may begin to feel they are interrupting or worse they are not wanted. Hey that smiling professional "How may I help you," it works for Wal-Mart and McDonalds and look how many customers they have and how long they've been around☺.

On the other hand if the BSE-Beauty Service Establishment looks busy, friendly and professional the potential client may walk in, stay and ask questions giving you the opportunity to service his or her needs. Remember your first days in Beauty School, the Milady Standard exam booklet chapter one speaks of the importance of the clean and neat appearance of the professional. Your professional station should be free of personal clutter such as food and drink containers, stains from food or drink, dirty towels, dust, dirty implements, an overflowing or dirty trash can with no trash bag. Too many family or client photos are also a common unprofessional mistake. The clients can barely see their new fly hairdo in the dirty smudged mirror for looking at dusty outdated, frayed photos. Get a small photo album to display your photos and the photos that your clients give you. Or perhaps put family photos neatly inside a cabinet door bulletin board style. Pictures of your children are adorable, your friends at the cruise partying in 1999 are all meaningful to you, but how does it connect to your clients? They are patronizing you to get beautiful and fly, not to look at your life 5 or 10 years ago.

Look around at your BSE. Yes even if you don't own it and especially if you do, is it truly a reflection of you? Invest in the physical appearance by starting with your own area in the BSE. What would you think of it as the first impression if you were a new client? What does your work area say about you? Are there hair filled combs, a half inch pile of dust bunnies, dried out nail polish bottles, disposable items that haven't' been disposed of yet lying about. A towel that has obviously never been replaced by the stain marks and dull "used to be light blue" now it has that 50 shades of grey frayed look. A towel should be replaced daily under any implements or product that are viewable to the public. Make it a priority to start or continue the better habit of being more organized and cleaner. This helps so much in maintaining a professional appearance throughout the day.

☝**Quote:** Mrs. Dorothy Avent, Client for over 40 years

I am a client of Mary Carver-Goldring. I met Mary and her five wonderful children when they moved to the Washington Metropolitan area from Tennessee. That was over 40 years ago. I was blessed to be amongst her first customers, God ordained this so. My 1st impressions of Mary was that she genuinely cares about people and as her client my hair and I would be treated well. I could not have asked for anything better than this. All of the family really love the Lord and exemplify it in their daily walk with God. I wish you all the best of the best and you and your entire family can say, "It pays to serve Jesus." To sum it all up, "Love never fails" 1 Corinthians 13:8

Thoughts/Ideas: _____

_____

_____

_____

_____

3. ALWAYS COMPLETE A FULL & THOROUGH CONSULTATION ON A CLIENTS FIRST VISIT.

Because ... When a client walks in you are setting the tone for all their future visits. Communicating effectively the first time will help them establish trust in their decision to choose you. Communication is so much easier if you have tools to make sure clients are getting the service they desire. Tools are extremely helpful in making sure clients get what they pay for. Your appreciative smile and confidence is the first tool. Knowing all about the products and services you offer, feeling confident in the products and answering your client's questions is the key to gaining and deserving their trust. The second tool is the CCIS-Client Consultation & Information Sheet we've provided in the back of this guide booklet as an essential tool. Hair Stylebooks, Pamphlets, Videos, Brochures and other tools can help as well.

The way to properly use the CCIS to begin that full and thorough consultation is to put the CCIS on a clipboard with a *working* ink pen. The CCIS is also a limited legal document for release of chemical services so that manual copy is great because you have your client's signature. Have your legal representation and/or insurance company review it to insure it is adequate for your business. As you present it to your client, explain that you need to gather important information to help you provide the best individualized service possible. It's a quick form and shouldn't be used simply to buy some time to do other things. Once your client completes it, review it and professionally decide what they need. If they have general needs great; however if they have specific problematic needs, be ready and suggest services that you are confident will solve problems and get results. As they ask questions be informed and offer them tools to help them choose.

✸ Ms. Mary's Personal Experience: *I once had a client apologize for being late, she had to drop her mother off at another salon that provided treatment for her mother's dry, damage and thinning hair. I was just dumbfounded. I was down right flabbergasted, because this was a long time client of mine. I told her I treat those issues, why didn't you just bring your mother to me I asked? The client stated to me that all my clients appeared to have healthy hair to which I was flattered but still confused that she hadn't even called to ask me how to deal with her mother's hair issue. When she realized my confusion, she clarified that when she took note of the condition of her mother's hair she had looked in the yellow pages (I'm telling my age) and found a Salon that treated dry, damaged and thinning hair. Her mother was around the corner at one of my colleague's salon being treated with the same products I would have used. I decided to put a note on my business card that stated, "I maintain and care for healthy hair/ treat and correct damaged hair." I also had brochures made outlining prices for these extra services I offered. The response from my long time clients was overwhelming; "I didn't know you offered these services," they stated to me. It was a wake up call for me and my old clients sent me new clients with hair and scalp issues.*

Think about your first doctor visit when they hand you that little clipboard with all the paperwork … *exactly!* It's a little annoying but you know you've got to do it and if your first appointment didn't begin that way you may start to wonder how professional that Doctors office really is. As a BSP it would be so unprofessional not to collect that vital information to do your job right! Salon Affairs offers you the CCIS-Client Consultation Information Survey. Think of it as that incredible chance to listen to your client's needs and why they are changing salons. You'll know why they need to pay to have this service *that they could very well do themselves* or go elsewhere to get it done. It's an essential tool for your arsenal of tools to communicate with your clients.

The consultation should begin after you review the CCIS with your client. You can then offer more effective solutions to solve problems or concerns your client is having. You can do this at any time with existing clients as well. Just let them know you are updating your files and while you're at it you want to make sure they are happy with the services you provide. **This tool, the CCIS is designed to help you do a thorough consultation** so that you can provide professional service. You need to know if the client is on medication, if they exercise, if they've had surgery lately, if they have a communicable disease etc to protect yourself and your other clients. This information is vital and will affect the professional service you provide.

✸ <u>Ms. Stella's Personal Experience</u>: *I once gave a client my personal favorite Walnut scrub during a pedicure only to have her start itching! I had failed to read her peanut allergy on the consultation card. Luckily she had her trusty Benadryl handy. "It was on the card you gave me to fill out," she told me later. I was so embarrassed that I hadn't even read the CCIS. It was a reminder to me that I have to follow the system that I had created. From that day forward I make sure to read each and every CCIS before I begin servicing the client. It's so easy to get comfortable in a bad habit.*

Other tools you should keep in good supply for that thorough consultation include clean, neat, and updated style books, brochures and pamphlets containing pictures and descriptions of all services that you provide. Many products will provide informative pamphlets for the products you use which you can give to client's undecided about their service choice. Be sure to read the pamphlet yourself so that when a client asks you for further information you can explain it to them. Also don't overwhelm your clients with a handful of pamphlets that don't support any of the needs they've addressed with you. It can be distracting, overwhelming and confusing. Treat your clients as individuals with specific attention to detail tailored to them.

Don't be afraid to ask clients if they are pleased. Go the extra mile to make sure to follow up with tools such as a post card to say,

"Glad you chose _____ Beauty Salon, look forward to seeing you again soon." That is a great way to follow up with clients and make sure they become repeat clients. If you don't want to send post cards, follow up with a quick phone call or email to say it and ask about the service, it's a chance to catch any bad experience in an effort to correct it.

Thoughts/Ideas: _____

_____

_____

_____

_____

_____

_____

_____

_____

_____

_____

_____

_____

_____

_____

_____

_____

_____

_____

_____

_____

_____

_____

_____

_____

4. I WILL HAVE A CONSULTATION WHEN GIVING A NEW SERVICE TO EXISTING CLIENTS.

Because ... A Consultation is Communication! Unfortunately many clients have been lost in the maze of bad experiences to ALL BSP's when not given the exact service they've requested with their Beauty Service Professionals. Also unfortunate is their previous BSP was not equipped to handle complaints, nor given the opportunity to correct or compensate for the missed communication or error. Therefore the disgruntled client is spreading malicious, nasty rumors about the entire industry not just that one ill equipped BSP. If the clients massage was too rough or too soft, their message to your potential clients could become, "it's not worth it to pay all that money and be roughed up or barely feel the benefits." If the color is too brassy or didn't cover the entire gray around the edges, the message could be "they don't know what they're doing I might as well do it myself or get my girlfriend to do it."

<u>Ms. Stella's Personal Experience</u>: Handling Complaints quickly and diplomatically. *When I worked in the retail industry, the corporate owners spent time and money training the staff to handle complaints because they knew the far reaching damage that could be done. Unhappy clients can wreak havoc on your business. We were taught to: listen with hands by our sides, sympathize with a caring expression then determine what the client wanted. When a client wants to complain, more often than not they simply want to be heard and acknowledged. I was surprised to learn they didn't want much else than that. Every so often they'd want 50% off an item or a coupon or something else. It's amazing how our initial defensive reaction can rise up when people begin to complain. But I learned to stop, listen and sympathized with the client's experience. I often got a smile half way through instead of the angry, upset face. I would then address the issue with the staff*

to make sure we were following customer service procedures. So remember to give a consultation to help avoid unhappy clients, but if you get a complaint be ready to handle it diplomatically.

The consultation should always be thorough leaving the client as well as the BSP feeling like they know what is expected. Feel free to use hair color tabs and any samples, pamphlets from and personal knowledge of the products distributor as well as style books to make sure everyone is on the right page. Always give your professional opinion if your gut is telling you what the client is asking for may not be the best choice for them. Find out their favorite scent and what scent they hate if giving a massage or a manicure using lotions and creams. Always strive to make sure their new service is as pleasurable, as beautiful and unforgettable as you possibly can. This will help you avoid complaints and unsatisfied clients most of the time.

✸ Ms. Mary's Personal Experience: *Dudley Products has an awesome tool, it's actually a Prescription pad with all their retail products listed on it with a check list. I used the tool with an existing client, after I asked that she share any concerns about her husband, daughter and sons hair. I was able to suggest at home products for them and send the products home with brochures designed just for them. She also purchased additional home hair care products for herself as she and her daughter don't share a bathroom she told me. That went from a $60 service to a $260 service plus retail once she purchased all the products. I quickly shared that with other stylist in my salon and began a bi-weekly contest to encourage my staff to sell more retail. Dudley product is in partnership with the professional stylist and I get great results and trust their products. You should only retail products you trust and have tried yourself.*

Remember, if your personal appearance is neat and up to date, it's easier to make suggestions as you gain the clients confidence and trust. Also please be honest with yourself, you are more confident as well when your own personal appearance is top notch. Give yourself a carefree easy everyday look that is easy to maintain so that you can look your best effortlessly.

✍**Quote: Kim Clark-Lewis, Cosmetologist**

"Working with the wonderful Mrs. Mary Carver Goldring, she shows me that everything God has brought her though and taught her, she is not afraid to share and help others. I have learned so much from her life. It has shown me that people are watching and can learn from my life experiences also."

Thoughts/Ideas: _____

_____

_____

_____

_____

_____

_____

_____

_____

_____

_____

_____

_____

_____

_____

_____

_____

_____

_____

_____

5. I WILL ALWAYS BE PROFESSIONAL ESPECIALLY WITH LONG TIME CLIENTS, RELATIVES AND FRIENDS.

Because … My clients, relatives and friends are the best *free* referral system! Advertising can be very expensive and it can be a challenge and somewhat difficult to find a proven marketing system that works. So, always be professional and do your best work consistently on your existing long time clients! They are walking billboards. They are alive and in living color texter's, Facebooker's, Insta-gramer's. They use Voxer, Tango, and take thousands of selfies, etc. They are walking postcards and business cards for your service and service establishments.

Your existing clients should always have two or three of your business cards on hand, that they are proud to share with people asking. If you give great, on time, quality service they should always be willing to add your name and phone number to that Facebook post or proudly pass on your business card. However if they are ashamed of the way they let you treat them, guess what? They will not let you treat their friends and family the way you treat them. For example if you are always late, giving excuse after excuse for your bad unprofessional behavior. Or after you've let them wait 30 minutes you now have to take a quick bite of lunch or talk on the phone or to a co-worker or friend right over your client's peaceful head, they couldn't imagine referring you to that trusted friend or family member. Or perhaps you consistently run long errands while your client is getting a service. The list goes on and on for what is considered unprofessional behavior. You must have some idea if you are a true UBSP- Unprofessional Beauty Service Person. You are surely aware of your bad habits. Whether it be Procrastination, consistently late, sloppy, unclean, unorganized, outdated skills.

Another reason to make it a good habit to be professional at all times is, just think about the fact that potential new clients are watching and listening for comments about a great BSP. Perhaps a client walks into the Salon to make a future first time appointment. They don't know when you're servicing your mother, your friend or a long time client. They are just watching to see how you treat your clients. They probably walked by and cased the salon out or asked around, they may already have a first impression. Let's pretend your name is "Susie." Just think how detrimental it is to your professional future if you are wearing an invisible tag that says, "Don't ask for Susie you'll regret it"!

✸ Mary's Personal Testimony: *As I sat waiting for my client to dry, I watched helplessly as my co-worker's client sat in the waiting area anxiously watching the parking lot for her stylist to arrive. This was not the first time I witnessed this scene. As my eyes met the client's eyes she said, "I don't know why I let her treat me this way, my money is green too." I smiled a reassuring smile because I had watched this scene play out many times previously. The client stated how she starts to feel stress on her way to the salon, which made my stomach ache for my beloved profession. The stylist arrived only to have a subway sandwich in hand. Just let me get a quick bite Ms. _____ and I'll be right with you she said to the client. No apology, just a glance of shame as the stylist rushed by. My eyes met the clients eyes again as she stood up and walked out the door in disgust as the stylist, who was thirty minutes late for the appointment hurried to the back to take a quick bite of her sandwich.*

Previously I had spoken with the stylist and shared my concerns to a shoulder shrug and a heartfelt, "I try to be on time, I really do." I had also spoken to the client about taking her on, or at least getting her started as I was always free at the time of her service. She was faithful to the stylist; she had known her for several years, following her from salon to salon and being thoroughly satisfied with her end result. The client said no to my offer, telling me (she), the stylist will be very upset with me if I let you do my hair, I've asked her and threatened her with letting you do my hair. She told me you have enough clients, she needs more clients." To that the client and I both laughed nervously. However I talked with the stylist about it later to which she replied, do you want to take all my clients? No! I replied it seems like you want to give them to me with your terrible unprofessional behavior and habits. I told her you make our entire industry look bad. Please try to do better I pleaded! That and many other scenarios, situations and conversations inspired me to write this guide booklet.

What does professional mean to you, what does professional look like to you? Think about it. Professional means using your inside professional voice, being calm and respectful in conducting business. Key words, **conducting business**. Yes, sure your personality is loud, brass and fun-loving ready to party! Don't overshadow your clients' needs for your service by refusing to tame your loud brass social personality. Develop a business personality. Perhaps you're easy going, shy and laid back. Don't be too shy to ask your clients questions that benefit their service from you. If you are louder than average that is your social personal personality. You should have a business personality. To conduct business you need to be aware of opportunities that create a profit for you. You also need to be aware of the missed opportunities that cause you to lose money. Profit and Loss are the two essential keys to business. You need to be poised to ask questions, you need to be ready to listen to responses. Also you need to be open and observant of client's moods, responses and demeanor for the service you are providing.

Be aware of the professional environment and the people paying you for your service. Greet clients with a smile ready to be of service to their needs. This should become a standard habit easily managed no matter what your mood is on any given day. Relatives, friends and long term clients (who become like friends) still need to know they are valued as paying clients. After all their money is green too! New and existing clients should not feel slighted with the attention and warmth you give to your family and long time existing clients.

When dealing with your long time clients, relatives and friends, they can become so comfortable that they feel like they are at home. They can begin to make a mess, invading other's comfortable space even acting territorial to you and your place of work. Let your relatives and friends know that you expect the same respect from them as you would give them if you happened to visit them at their place of employment. As a rule, relatives and friends should not be allowed to browse your place of employment and invade other co-worker's space and privacy. Nor should they "hangout" around you as you service other clients. It may be a fun ritual for you and your clients however ask yourself is it respectful to your other clients or your co-workers clients. For that fun, gather round lets catch up time … Plan a fun girl's pizza night to catch up, leave your professional environment just that! Professional.

Face it, some of your clients (especially women) are not capable of demanding, showing or telling you how to R.E.S.P.E.C.T. or treat them in a professional way. However, some are better at this than others. The stress of being taken advantage of or being taken for granted is a threat to your business. Put yourself in your client's situation. If you don't think it's easy to speak up for yourself; perhaps you are among the BSP's having difficulty demanding respect in your pricing, time and courtesy. Perhaps you need to tell a busy body client something or perhaps your client smells bad. How do you tell them? Your clients may want to tell you something as well. That is why professionalism is an art and a skill that needs constant attention. It can be learned and developed if it becomes your goal. Sharpen your professional blade from time to time when it becomes dull. If this sounds like Salon Affairs is suggesting you become a BSP who is stuffy, phony and pretentious you've got it all wrong. A BSP is on time, well read in his or her art and skilled in their craft. Supplies are plentiful, appointments are respected and clients feel valued by their BSP. Your natural effervescent personality is an added bonus to those attributes of professionalism.

◀))) **Think about this** …

If you are having difficulty controlling clients, a sign with the salon price list, rules and regulations posted large and in a promenate location will help. Also a brochure containing the rules, prices and amenities given at that initial consultation is a great way to establish that desired and lasting first impression. Let the sign or brochure become a "silent sales tool." Work your courage and your nerve up to let clients know what you need as well as opening the door and providing tools from them to tell you what they need.

★Also if you choose to give your BFF or family (blood relatives) a discount, make it an amount or percentage off a service that doesn't mean you will not make any profit. You could easily actually end up paying your BFF for the service with your supplies and labor. Make their appointment time when it is convenient for you, on a slow day or afternoon. Reserve the right to change it if a full service client needs that time slot. Give your full service clients prime time appointments. It's easy to get burned out with friends and relatives who take advantage of your kindness.

☝Quote: Jackie Perry, Client for over 30 years

"I have been Mary Carver-Goldring's customer for over 32 years. Mary is not only my beautician but she is also my friend. When a friend or acquaintance would see my hair style they always asked the question, "who did your hair?" Many customers have been referred to her through someone else and they continue to go to her shop today because they are very pleased with her care and service. When one of her clients has a need to get service on a certain day (or change their regular appointment) in order to attend the funeral of a family member or friend, to make an unexpected trip out of town, etc., Mary has come in many times on her days off in order to accommodate them. Mary always pays extra special care to her customers' needs and desires. I have and will always continue to refer customers to Mary."

☝**Quote: Dr. Helen C. Scott-Carter, Client for 25 Years**

"It is with delight that I give a testimony to the wonderful care I have received for 25 years from the hands of the "Hair Doctor," Ms. Mary Carver Goldring. Her care of my hair needs pales in the genuine concern she has had for me through the years. Thanks seems so inadequate for the manner in which she treats her clients. Each client is special and important to her and she gives her undivided attention to each one."

Thoughts/Ideas: _____

_____
_____
_____
_____
_____
_____
_____
_____
_____
_____
_____
_____
_____
_____
_____
_____

6. DO UNTO OTHERS AS YOU WOULD HAVE THEM DO UNTO YOU.

Because ... When you go to a restaurant, doctor's office or your bank you expect professional timely and good quality service. If you get to the supermarket and the shelves are empty or they consistently don't have what's on your list what will you do? Think of other places you frequent like the gym or church even. Equally important you expect quality products, clean surroundings and an informed staff of employees. Ask yourself this question; why do I continue to frequent these places and choose these service professional? When you patronize these places, if you don't receive what you are paying your hard earned money for; there are several others providing the same service at locations conveniently located within minutes. Competition in the Beauty Service Industry is stiff. Give your clients the same quality service you expect. Holding a license for professional service means you are qualified to dispense information and you have a skill that is in demand. Be mindful the next time you are in a position to receive a service, relate that to how your clients feel when waiting for you to service them.

✌Quote: Karen Taylor, Cosmetologist

"My Aunt Mary inspired me to become a cosmetologist when I was a young woman. Watching her at work with her clients and later working with her in the salon was a big influence on me. Her skills and experiences as a cosmetologist are outstanding. I have always told my clients that my Aunt has paved the way for me. I strive to be like her. I thank God for the person she is. When I hear this scripture, Matthew 5:16 being read, I think of my Aunt Mary. "Let your light shine before men, that they may see your good deeds and glorify your father in heaven."

Thoughts/Ideas: _____

_____

_____

_____

_____

_____

_____

_____

_____

_____

_____

_____

_____

_____

_____

_____

_____

_____

_____

_____

_____

_____

_____

_____

_____

_____

_____

7. ALWAYS RESPECT YOUR CLIENT'S TIME.

Because … When time is lost it cannot be regained and people are very sensitive about wasting time. You will hear a lot about time in this guide booklet because it is one of the primary reasons you will loose clients. Time will be a recurring overlapping theme in this booklet or had you not noticed☺.

So many personal and professional lessons learned from experiences prompted and inspired this guide booklet. Experiences have included over the years, issues with clients making appointments and not keeping them or not rescheduling, times of sitting with no one to service yet bills to pay. As a salon owner I soon realized if my stylist weren't making money I was in deep trouble as well. When I worked at salons over the years, it didn't seem to be my problem that my co-workers weren't making money or they may not be as professional as I had become. However, when I became salon owner I couldn't afford to allow stylist to give my salon a bad reputation, or sit making no money. In the early days when I went from stylist, to manager, to salon owner I learned so much. As I learned I wanted to share but quickly learned not everyone is teachable or want to hear what you've learned.

Some of the most important lessons I've learned from stylists who decided to leave my salon: It always seemed a rush decision to leave as the grass seemed much greener at the Salon down the street. There weren't as many rules at that salon, so they'd been told by their fellow Beauty Service Professional friends. However; as I sat with my stylists during their exit interview to discuss why they may want to leave the salon, most of the time it was because their client list was dwindling. On one such instance when a stylist was in complete denial about her habits contributing to this problem, we decided to create an anonymous salon survey box for her final two weeks at the salon. That was an eye opener for everyone. We learned one stylist spits when she talks, the stylist leaving talks on the phone too much and always showed up late to appointments yet wanted to rush the job at the end of the day. The clients didn't like the staff to clean the floor and the salon with the same towels used on their hair. They suggested magazines and asked for items to be added to retail.

When we compiled what this particular stylist clients had to say, it became a dreaded exit interview because it's always difficult or a challenge to bring up professionalism to adults. The reason we say dreaded above is also because, it's a challenge to look at what we may be doing to contribute to our problems. Yet it has to be done because we need to know when we need to get out of our own way when it comes to succeeding. Included in the BSP Assistant's Handbook in a copy of the exit interview for staff leaving the BSE voluntarily or if fired.

Over the years, each time we review the salon survey's the most popular comment we receive are on the subject of time. Some clients were bold enough to put their names on their survey and thanked us for the opportunity to share their thoughts. Others chose to return it anonymously when they complained about one stylist or the salon. You can be sure we were prepared to address those complaints immediately. Included with the Salon Survey Cards are instructions how to respond to client complaints and concerns.

Also in reviewing the CCIS–Client Information Sheet Tool responses for new and existing clients over the years we've noticed that they list time as being a reason to change salons quiet often. When clients run late it can throw the whole day off. It can seem like someone always has to be somewhere that day and as a result time is always a juggle if you don't have those set rules in place to manage it. As we've stated earlier communication goes a long way. Always be prepared and consistent in your message about time.

Communication about your "Time Policy" should be listed on your brochure, newsletter and also posted prominently so your clients will be aware and can adhere to it. The policy should be strictly enforced consistently for all clients if it is a strict rule. I have patronized larger Salons or fully booked busy Spa's that have a policy that states, "fifteen minutes late and you have to reschedule." A late client may also forfeit their deposit. It's a great incentive for clients to be on time; however it can be a win/loose for some clients. It also has the potential to be a loose/loose for smaller salons that try that policy. When I've visited full service spa's I've notice that the voice mail states the policy, it's on the end of the receipt and I was reminded of the policy once again when the Spa called the day prior to remind me of my scheduled appointment. That is a strictly enforced policy.

In a smaller salon or start up spa you may give clients more options if they are late. The key is communicate it to the client. They may have to be worked in-between other clients that were on time. With a reassuring smile, remind them of the salon policy and then kindly point out amenities giving them several suggestions of things they can do while they are waiting if they *choose* to wait or come back later. Remember and be aware that if they leave upset or choose not to wait they may go to spend their money somewhere else. Thinking like a BSP, is it better to service the client well or risk loosing them to another establishment? When a client runs late and you have a cancelled appointment an hour or two away, ask them if they mind returning in two hours? Always give clients options. Perhaps they were getting an hour Swedish massage. Maybe they could get a thirty minute deep tissue instead for the same price. If you are wise and business savvy, you can make the same amount of money for a shorter service time and everyone is happy. A win/win depending on who you ask☺.

Most importantly as a BSP-beauty service professional, be committed and *"don't be a part of the problem"* by scheduling too closely, being late to start your day or taking long lunch breaks and running errands in between clients. Time management is a valuable skill for the BSP. Make the wait less painful by providing updated magazines, books and a clean comfortable low stress atmosphere so the wait isn't compounded by a lack of things to do while the clients wait. A wait can be excruciating if the atmosphere is dirty with old and outdated torn reading material. Uncomfortable chairs, a loud television, children running and not using their inside voice to name a few issues. As you've learned reading this guide booklet, these issues can be addressed.

In addition to your main waiting area with a television, children and folks talking loud on the phone or working on laptops, create 2nd waiting area dedicated to quiet and relaxation if you have space. This quiet area may play soft music, provide space for reading and relaxing. Create a children's area with activity and coloring books. Give a prize of candy or $1 off a movie for well behaved children at the end of the visit. Take the opportunity to teach children and their uninformed parents that in a business we must use our inside voice and conduct ourselves as citizens in public, not at home. Just remember to brainstorm because problems have solutions. If you never acknowledge your problems you will never think of a solution. If your gut first impression of our GB examples above sound corny, or unrealistic then these are not right for you but trust me, there are solutions that will be right for your environment.

Also a snack machine is a great source of revenue when freshly and consistently stocked as well as a waiting room treat when clients want a quick snack to last until lunch or dinner. You could also use that as an incentive offering clients or their children a free snack as a reward if you are running a little behind schedule or when children behave well.

We must let clients know when we are running excessively late and if it's not a routine experience the clients will understand and usually choose not to complain. However if it is a common experience to have to wait more than fifteen minutes for their service to begin, problems will arise from your clients. If it takes you two hours for a basic service that should take one hour your clients will begin to look elsewhere or not refer any clients or worse speak negatively of the establishment to other people waiting or coming in for service. This is a bad reflection on the entire service establishment if a client leaves spreading nasty rumors about the service or their wait time.

Whatever your field or profession, there are average time and service guidelines for the services you provide. Take some time to actually become aware of when your client walks through the door and what time it is when they are leaving. Then simply ask yourself if you are doing your best to honor your client's precious time.

Thoughts/Ideas: _____

_____

_____

_____

_____

_____

_____

_____

8. BE SURE YOUR STERILIZATION, SANITATION & ROUTINE CLEANLINESS PRACTICES ARE UP TO DATE.

Because ... Simply Stated, your State Board requires it. It's the law for your client and your own protection. When you maintain safe sanitary practices, you feel more professional and confident. Make it a standard everyday habit to keep up with the current laws, rules and regulations for your state. Keep yourself and your clients safe from the spread of disease and infections. Please do yourself the professional courtesy and lower your stress level by following the rules set forth by the State Board of licensing for your profession.

Make sure to routinely wash all materials that come in contact with your client's clothes and person. Your styling capes, robes, linen and shampoo capes should be routinely washed and kept in good repair. Clean the Velcro of hair and cotton to keep it closing and functioning properly. If there is a small tear or large dye stain on any cape, it's time to trash that item. It could become small squares to clean the salon or trash.

When is the last time you've cleaned your massage tray, roller tray or makeup tray. Look at it now. If your first impressionable thought is yuck! Then it's time to take everything off/out and clean it. You can wash your magnetic rollers in the washing machine once you've freed them of clips, end papers and pins. How often do you wash those make up brushes? Remember that bottle spilled last month and each time you take out a bottle from the facial tray it sticks to the bottom of the basket. Do you think your client doesn't notice how dirty and disorderly your tray, cabinet or draws are? While you are talking about nothing, they are looking at your dirty work environment. Don't wait for that State Board visit to clean your work environment.

Keep it cleaned daily. It really doesn't add much time to your routine to do any of these steps.

Hiring and thoroughly training assistants can make cleaning, and professional attention to detail an easy way to manage this chore. Thoroughly train your assistants on everything "State Board" requires. Let them know this has to be done per state board. Make it the assistants, staff and employees responsibility to keep the standard of the establishment up to your State Board standards. Included in the back of the GB you'll find a sample check list found in the BSP Assistants Handbook. You can post the lists so they can easily refer to it often when they are … bored. Or give them a check list daily that they can return to the owner/manager(s) before they leave. The lines at the bottom of the check list are so that you can add any work that must be done that day.

Walk around your establishment and you'll find many things to add to their scope of work. If you find an assistant texting or slouching in a chair during their hours of work, it's a bad reflection of your ability to mange them. Whose fault is it if it continues? Employees need to be managed, trained, reprimanded and rewarded. Get a system in place to handle this aspect of your business.

Assistants are an extension of your professionalism. They are a reflection of you. For example, if they hear a client coughing, they should quickly respond with a cup of water or even pointing to a candy dish filled with starlight mints and cough drops which is so much better than ignoring the cough. If you're running late, they can communicate that to the client and point out salon amenities. Periodic checks of the waiting room to pick up debris, straiten magazines, clean and sweep are all apart of their daily responsibilities. They can purge magazines and make sure you have the previous two month copies only, not the entire twelve month torn frayed copies from the last year of Cosmo. Just think, you can use the old magazines to make your goal chart, give them to the local laundry mat, or simply trash them.

Keeping the BSE–Beauty Service Establishment State Board certifiably clean, neat and orderly is a top ten on the BSP's list of things to do. Whether it's that State Board representative walking through the door of the establishment, or any new or returning client as well, that first impression will impact their visit.

Thoughts/Ideas: _____

_____

_____

_____

_____

_____

_____

_____

_____

_____

_____

_____

_____

_____

_____

_____

_____

_____

_____

_____

_____

9. KEEP YOUR TRADE SUPPLIES IN STOCK AND TRADE TOOLS IN GOOD REPAIR.

Because … It's an investment in you and your business. When you run out of trade supplies it is frustrating, stressful and unprofessional. Your confidence suffers, how you feel when you realize you are out of something should prevent you from running out. How often does it happen?

If you are a booth renter, an employee or a freelance service provider make sure that your supplies needed for the day are in stock and tools for service are in good repair. As a BSP routinely look at your appointments for the next week, or even the day before to ensure you have what you need for those clients. When you run out of hair color, relaxer, massage oil, nail polish remover, towels, clean combs, capes, robes etc. it can be so frustrating, stressful and depressing. For you and your client. Your confidence will suffer and as a result your clients will feel unimportant and silently question their decision to put up with it. Check their eye movement and posture when you complain out loud or cringe at the fact that you don't have the hair color they've been so excited to get. How do you feel when a client walks to the front desk to purchase that finishing spray, nail polish, hand lotion for their vacation and you have to say, "We're out of that"? Ugh! So easily corrected with planning.

Do you know this person, or worse are you this person? Always borrowing items, stealing supplies, using your fellow BSP's tools because you haven't been disciplined enough to purchase yours or replace the one you've carelessly broken because you don't carefully put it away each time you borrow it? When you do this your professional relationships will suffer. Are you running out before each client, luckily the beauty supply is just a few doors down, no harm in running out before each client to purchase what you need, right? Wrong! It's more expensive, it's not good time management, and it's not the way to properly or successfully manage your business and get the most profitable return on your investment.

If you do the math, say you purchase wholesale from a supplier a large box of color rinse. You pay $50.00 you do 50 people. You run get 1 bottle from the beauty supply down the street at $5.00 per bottle, pay retail for 1 person when you realize you ran out of color. That's $5.00 per person retail instead of the $1.00 per person if you purchase it wholesale. $4.00 loss on each person will really add up over the year. Take time and do the math on your profit or loss when paying retail.

If you need help getting organized and running your business more professionally seek it. Take a business course at the local community college. Make sure to attend local and area trade shows. Pay for those trade show classes they offer for more than just the tax write off. Don't just stand in front of the new product stands watching some fancifully stylist whipping up that blue hair with sparkles, while you take cell phone pictures. Go to a business class, take time to ask some of the celebrity BSP's some questions. Get your money's worth out of that trade show. You can also seek help closer to home, seek help from the BSE owner, manager or other BSP's who seem to be proficient in what you are lacking. The only really, really stupid question is the one you don't ask when you honestly don't know the answer. The only thing known to man is that he doesn't know everything and wasn't born doing everything well. Ask for help from people trained in the skill you are lacking.

Your local trade supplier is a wealth of information and networking as well. Give them some business cards just in case a frantic shopper needs s new BSP. Take advantage of their special deals and offers for new product, visit their websites and join coupon email lists if they have them.

Guess what you've scored some points by purchasing this GB-Guide Booklet. Hopefully you are not borrowing a copy because you need to take notes in your own booklet and so does the person whose guide booklet you are holding if it's not yours. There are copies of the checklists that need to be made by the owner. You'll need to refer to this guide booklet again and again and track your improvement. So purchase your very own copy and one for that co-worker whose face keeps popping up as you read the 10 Key Points. Hide your copy from them. Give yourself the key's to unlock your success.

⚘**Quote:** Mary Overton, Dudley Products Sales Rep.

"I've been Mary Goldring's Dudley Products representative for about 18 years. She has travelled and attended our trade shows, seminars, product knowledge classes and our EMS-Educational Motivational Symposiums for many years. She has given presentations at seminars to over 30 Cosmetologist and students and has encouraged them to be professional at all times and to learn how to gain a good customer base and retain them."

⚘**Quote:** Ken Williams, Owner Action Beauty Supply.

"It is with great pride that I endorse Ms. Mary Carver' Goldring's book. In fact I've encouraged her to write one for several years to help struggling Stylists and Salons. I've known Mary as a successful community business owner who has patronized my trade supply business for more than 25 years. She has travelled to Trade Shows on my bus trips, and supported any product education I've offered.

I have referred my valued customers to her knowing that they will be serviced professionally. I'm sure she will share all her knowledge, holding nothing back because that is just the kind, encouraging and supportive type of professional that she is."

Thoughts/Ideas: _____

_____

_____

_____

_____

_____

_____

_____

_____

_____

_____

_____

_____

_____

_____

_____

_____

_____

_____

_____

_____

_____

_____

_____

_____

10. ALWAYS DO YOUR VERY BEST, NO MATTER WHO THE CLIENT IS.

Because ... This is THE key! Each of the previous nine Keys summarized lead to this final and 10th key. ALWAYS do your very best, no matter who the client is. Clients will become so secure in knowing that they've made a great decision choosing you as their BSP out of all the hundreds they could have chosen. Your clients will easily refer clients to you having confidence that their friends, relatives, strangers and co-workers won't think they are crazy for putting up with your unprofessional behavior. To do your best you need to be at your best. Be Healthy, Wise and Wealthy in Spirit as well as finances. It is key to maintaining your health, don't overwork your body, eat properly and get rest so that you can enjoy the fruits of your labor. Be Wise. Wisdom is acquired through actively seeking solutions, reflection and monitoring your growth throughout your life. Ask for help; seek out mentors who are where you want to be. Wealthy, financially and emotionally are equally important. Seeking and getting professional tax help, money management, financial planning and retirement strategies are all extremely key in this our BSP environment.

To our entire fellow family of BSP's, we want you to know that our desire for you in writing this GB is to help you actively strengthen your weaknesses, refine and sharpen your strengths with the goal of learning and improving until the day you die. As you learn and grow be sure to reach back and inspire positive change in others. Be your best self, live your best life ... Your spirit will rejoice!

Final Encouraging words about the 10 Key Points

These are the 10 Key Points to Building and Keeping a Good Clientele. Over the course of my 50 year career as a Cosmetologist,

Manager and then Business Owner, I was repeatedly asked by many suppliers and other stylist how I consistently kept a healthy satisfied clientele. The question was asked so often especially during the many recessions I've personally lived through, that I started to write down what I thought I was doing right. I became serious about it after the following true story:

"Once I called a supplier with a product order and it seemed that literally I heated and began eating my lunch only to look up and see the supplier's delivery person opening the door. "Wow that was fast," I told the young man. "No one is busy Ms. Mary, you know we are in a recession," he reminded me. "Well everyone is suffering except for you I think," he told me. "I don't know what you are doing Ms. Mary, but it's working," he said. We laughed and that young man said, "You need to write a book it seems that you always have clients no matter when I deliver to you, even in the middle of the day." As I laughed, it dawned on me that he was telling the truth and I should share my basic rules for success. I was finding myself alone with my clients in the salon more often lately I thought to myself"

My advice to you is to let this GB-Guide Booklet be a guide. Read the 10 key points often, again and again and again once more, so they become apart of your professional ethics. See them as a key that will unlock any and all doors. If you haven't already, I strongly encourage you to do the self-evaluation and actively seek to improve and become the best BSP-Beauty Service Professional you can be. There is always room for improvement in whatever field you are in. There is absolutely, positively no excuse … not inflation, location or situation for not having a full clientele. People will always need to have professional services performed and they will make a way to meet those needs. You need only listen, be sensitive to the needs and learn how to supply the demand.

I dare you to unlock your potential for success.

Self-Evaluation, Self-Correction Pop Quiz

👍 BE Honest, BE Brave, BE Courageous BE You!

Right now in this very moment ... are you remembering the anxiety you felt back in grade school when the teacher boldly and loudly walked in and announced, "POP Quiz"! It took you by surprise; you started to wonder if you remembered anything you'd been taught. You felt dread in your gut and hoped this didn't count so much toward the final grade. Or perhaps you'd been studying, had good habits and felt confident you would nail the pop quiz with an easy A+. Well this is a self-quiz you can't fail. Just breath deeply answer honestly and get ready to learn some thing's about yourself that you may not have been aware of. The best part, you'll get another chance later to take it again

(Take BEFORE you read The Booklet)

My *Self Evaluation* AND *Self Correction* Pop Quiz

1. PROFESSIONALISM

Y N   I wear clean, comfortable and relevant to my profession, attire everyday?

Y N   Is the smock or uniform that I wear neat, clean and pristine? (No rips, not torn or frayed)

Y N   Are my hair, skin and nails representative of my profession?

Y N   I smile and greet my clients by name and communicate with them about their needs each appt.?

Y N   Is my license current, hanging prominently with a current picture attached? (Not expired or revoked)

Y N   Could I easily pass a State Board Inspection on most days?

2. MARKETING/ADVERTISING

Y N   I have current Client Information including: name, address, email, cell phone, home phone, work phone for all my clients?

Y N   I have a large supply of current business cards on hand?

Y N   Are there currently at least 10 clean business cards in my possession every day everywhere I go?

Y N   Are my postcards/ brochures and price list updated neat and in good supply?

Y N   Are my advertisement, referral, and marketing strategies effective? (No) if you don't have a Strategy.

Y N   I update my professional Social Media (Facebook, twitter, insta-gram) page often. Make sure to offer coupons and incentives at least monthly.

Y N   My Professional Social Media page is separate from my personal page.

Y N   Is my business resume current?

Y N   I have all the clients I can handle; there is no room for not five or ten more.

3. TIME: ROUTINELY (80% OR MORE OF THE TIME)

Y N   I arrive 30 minutes or more before my clients are scheduled?

Y N   I don't run errands often between clients leaving them to finish sitting waiting for my return?

Y N   I schedule a consistent day off so I don't frequently have to reschedule clients to be off.

Y N   I take my lunch and dinner break so it doesn't inconvenience my clients?

Y N   I frequently arrive 10 or more minutes after my clients arrive.

4. KNOWLEDGE

Y N   Am I confident in answering any questions my clients ask relevant to my profession?

Y N   When clients ask a question I can quickly and easily find the answer if I don't know the answer?

Y N   I have solutions for common issues my clients ask about, they trust me?

Y N   I have current education and up to date knowledge of various remedies to achieve solutions?

Y N   I attend classes and or read updated literature on current trends at least once a week?

5. SKILL AND TECHNIQUE

Y N   When looking at the latest trend books, I can perform most techniques well, in my profession?

Y N   I feel confident and comfortable when clients ask me about most techniques?

Y N   I seek education and practice on techniques I don't feel comfortable performing?

Y N   Have I tried to learn and perfect a new technique within the last month?

Y N   Have I tried to learn and perfect a new technique within the 6 months?

Y N   Have I tried to learn and perfect a new technique within the past year?

6. CONTINUED EDUCATION

Y N   I attend out of state trade shows at least once a year?

Y N   I subscribe to and read a relevant professional magazine monthly?

Y N   I attend local classes at least twice a year?

Y N   I attend classes and seek professional coaching for areas of weakness that I have?

7. PERSONAL & SERVICE

Y N   Would I choose me to perform the service I offer?

Y N   Knowing what I know about me, I am 90% or 100% on top of my profession?

Y N   I'm proud and satisfied of the way I treat my professional career?

Y N   I'm proud and satisfied of the way I treat my clients?

Y N   90%-100% of my clients are thoroughly satisfied with the way I handle their trust in me?

Y N   True? My clients would not leave me if they had an easier option presented to them?

Y N   I truly enjoy coming to work 90% -100% of the time?

Y N   I save 10% or more of my income?

Y N   I have an IRA or other retirement plan?

Y N   I am making the amount of money I feel I'm worth?

Y N   My clients pay more for my service as I increase the price at the rate of inflation?

Y N   50% of my clients refer new clients to me regularly.

8. BUSINESS

Y N   I use quick books or another business accounting software to keep my business affairs in order?

Y N   I have an accountant, CPA or CFA that manages my business monthly.

Y N   I have an accountant, CPA or CFA advises me about my business.

Y N   I have sought the advice of an accountant, CPA or CFA?

Y N   True? Near that tax filing deadline, I'm confident organized and ready to file?

Y N   False? Near that tax filing deadline, I get physically stressed thinking and dreading filing taxes?

Y N   I pay quarterly estimated taxes to offset paying at the end of the year?

Y N   These questions sound expensive but I can't afford not to do the things to make my business easier.

Now that wasn't so bad … or was it? You've heard the popular quote, "today is the first day of the rest of your life"? Well it is. Today or right now in fact is a moment that you can decide to turn it all around or keep heading in the direction you are going.

✴ Ms. Stella's personal Experience: *I remember my first review as a paid professional. I was instantly reflective about my work as I knew the 'Review Day' approached. I was delighted when my manager walked in, handed me a self-evaluation and told me to be honest with myself and that it was for my eyes only. He stated that he would be interested to know how and what I felt needed improvement. It was a huge relief to me, I was probably much harder on myself than the manager could or would have been.*

Any quiz, especially this quiz is just a simple tool to see if you're learning. Are you learning life's important lessons, are you learning from your mistakes or looking back with regret or worse still repeatedly making the same mistakes of the past?

Taking a self-evaluation quiz can help the optimist see if they're on track in their career and give them an opportunity to give themselves a pat on the back. The pessimist may decide, wow I'm a big fat failure and there is no hope for me. The right or best response to this self evaluation, pop quiz is to think positive! Think about the areas you identify as needing improvement. Pat yourself on the back for all the yes answers. For all the no answers, give yourself a big fat arms wrapped around yourself hug for being honest. Old habits are breakable once identified. See how they may be holding you back from being your best. You may have lost clients, you may have been afraid to increase prices due to a lack of skill. Your confidence may have suffered and may be the cause of some of those no answers. Everyone has room for improvement, it's a mouse trap full of not me cheese for anyone who doesn't believe that there is always a lesson to be learned.

You see from page one we asked, "Are you willing to pay the price for success?" No cutting corners or making excuses for your behavior. Take the bull by the horns! (Can you imagine that?) Well guess what, you are the bull! Look in the mirror, face yourself, and face your fears. Self-Motivated success starts with forming good habits that people who fail just don't want to do. You can't give in to your moods; you have to set standards for yourself that require accountability to you. Once those higher standards are set, see yourself working toward them, forming new, better habits and reaping the rewards and being proud that you made the choice to pay the price for success, not failure.

☝**Quote: Sharon Robinson, Senior Cosmetologist, Barber & Instructor**

"My Aunt Mary inspired me by leading by example. She took my hand so that I would do the same thing. I've achieved my Cosmetologist, Barbering and Instructor License. My Salon career had served me well and I decided to seek a BSP Instructor education. I've been able to inspire students as I teach them and watch them get their license in this awesome Beauty Industry. And for all the lesson I learned from my Aunt I am grateful!"

Thoughts/Ideas: _____

_____

_____

_____

_____

_____

_____

_____

(Take *BEFORE* you read The Booklet)

Self-Evaluation and Self-Correction Summary Sheet

BE Honest, BE Brave and BE Courageous!

1. Professionalism 6 questions. How many Yes? _____ How many No? _____

   How and what can I improve: _____

   _____

   _____

   What am I doing right: _____

   What I can change easily: _____

2. Marketing/Advertisement 9 questions. How many Yes? _____ How many No? _____

   How and what can I improve: _____

   _____

   _____

   What am I doing right: _____

   What I can change easily: _____

3. Time 5 questions. How many Yes? _____ How many No? _____

   How and what can I improve: _____

   _____

   _____

   What am I doing right: _____

   What I can change easily: _____

4. Knowledge 5 questions. How many Yes? _____ How many No? _____

How and what can I improve: _____

_____

_____

What am I doing right: _____

What I can change easily: _____

5. Skill & Technique 6 questions. How many Yes? _____ How many No? _____

How and what can I improve: _____

_____

_____

What am I doing right: _____

What I can change easily: _____

6. Continued Education 4 questions. How many Yes? _____ How many No? _____

How and what can I improve: _____

_____

_____

What am I doing right: _____

What I can change easily: _____

7. Personal & Service 12 questions. How many Yes? _____ How many No? _____

How and what can I improve: _____

_____

_____

What am I doing right: _____

What I can change easily: _____

8. Business 7 questions. How many Yes? _____ How many No?

_____

How and what can I improve: _____

_____

_____

What am I doing right: _____

What I can change easily: _____

Talley your honest answers to the 54 Self-Evaluation questions.

Total Yes Answers_____ Total NO Answers _____

SCORE YOURSELF AS FOLLOWS FOR THE TOTAL YES ANSWERS.

A+ 51-54

A+ 51-52 A 48-50 B 44-47 C39-43 D 30-38 F-29 OR BELOW

75% (40) OF MY 54 ANSWERS WERE NO! (NO'S ARE NOT SO GOOD)

T F   I know I need to change but I don't know where to begin.

T F   I'm failing in my career, I've been thinking about a career change but I love this one.

T F   I don't think I'm the problem, the economy is bad, it's the salon owners fault but it's not my fault.

T F   I have bad adult habits that need to be improved, I lack motivation to improve.

T F   I'm not smart enough to improve, I lack focus.

T F   This profession is not a lucrative career for anyone except celebrity beauty service professionals.

The problem/excuse is: _____

_____

What I can change easily: _____

_____

75% (40) OF MY 54 ANSWERS WERE YES! (YES'S ARE GOOD)

T F   I've always been a type A, do my best, improve where I can, self-correct type of person.

T F   I've had a great mentor or coach in the profession that has guided my career.

T F   I read self help books to stay motivated and focused. Failure is not an option for me.

T F   I'm planning to take my career to the next level, learn more techniques and ask for more money.

T F   There is room for improvement in the _____ area, I was surprised or not by that.

   What I'm doing right: _____

   _____

   Where there's room for improvement: _____

   _____

   _____

After My *Self Evaluation* AND *Self Correction* Pop Quiz

1. PROFESSIONALISM

Y N   I wear clean, comfortable and relevant to my profession, attire every day?

Y N   Is the smock or uniform that I wear neat, clean and pristine? (No rips, not torn or frayed)

Y N   Are my hair, skin and nails representative of my profession?

Y N   I smile and greet my clients by name and communicate with them about their needs each appt.?

Y N   Is my license current, hanging prominently with a current picture attached? (Not expired or revoked)

Y N   Could I easily pass a State Board Inspection on most days?

2. MARKETING/ADVERTISING

Y N   I have current Client Information including: name, address, email, cell phone, home phone, work phone for all my clients?

Y N   I have a large supply of current business cards on hand?

Y N   Are there currently at least 10 clean business cards in my possession every day everywhere I go?

Y N   Are my postcards/ brochures and price list updated neat and in good supply?

Y N   Are my advertisement, referral, and marketing strategies effective? (No) if you don't have a Strategy.

Y N   I update my professional Social Media (Facebook, Twitter, Insta-gram) page often. Make sure to offer coupons and incentives at least monthly.

Y N   My Professional Social Media page is separate from my personal page.

Y N   Is my business resume current?

Y N   I have all the clients I can handle; there is no room for not five or ten more.

3. TIME: ROUTINELY (80% OR MORE OF THE TIME)

Y N   I arrive 30 minutes or more before my clients are scheduled?

Y N   I don't run errands often between clients leaving them to finish sitting waiting for my return?

Y N   I schedule a consistent day off so I don't frequently have to reschedule clients to be off.

Y N   I take my lunch and dinner break so it doesn't inconvenience my clients?

Y N   I frequently arrive 10 or more minutes after my clients arrive.

4. KNOWLEDGE

Y N   Am I confident in answering any questions my clients ask relevant to my profession?

Y N   When clients ask a question I can quickly and easily find the answer if I don't know the answer?

Y N   I have solutions for common issues my clients ask about, they trust me?

Y N   I have current education and up to date knowledge of various remedies to achieve solutions?

Y N   I attend classes and or read updated literature on current trends at least once a week?

5. SKILL AND TECHNIQUE

Y N   When looking at the latest trend books, I can perform most techniques well, in my profession?

Y N I feel confident and comfortable when clients ask me about most techniques?

Y N I seek education and practice on techniques I don't feel comfortable performing?

Y N Have I tried to learn and perfect a new technique within the last month?

Y N Have I tried to learn and perfect a new technique within the 6 months?

Y N Have I tried to learn and perfect a new technique within the past year?

6. CONTINUED EDUCATION

Y N I attend out of state trade shows at least once a year?

Y N I subscribe to and read a relevant professional magazine monthly?

Y N I attend local classes at least twice a year?

Y N I attend classes and seek professional coaching for areas of weakness that I have?

7. PERSONAL & SERVICE

Y N Would I choose me to perform the service I offer?

Y N Knowing what I know about me, I am 90% or 100% on top of my profession?

Y N I'm proud and satisfied of the way I treat my professional career?

Y N I'm proud and satisfied of the way I treat my clients?

Y N 90%–100% of my clients are thoroughly satisfied with the way I handle their trust in me?

Y N True? My clients would not leave me if they had an easier option presented to them?

Y N I truly enjoy coming to work 90% –100% of the time?

Y N   I save 10% or more of my income?

Y N   I have an IRA or other retirement plan?

Y N   I am making the amount of money I feel I'm worth?

Y N   My clients pay more for my service as I increase the price at the rate of inflation?

Y N   50% of my clients refer new clients to me regularly.

8. BUSINESS

Y N   I use quick books or another business accounting software to keep my business affairs in order?

Y N   I have an accountant, CPA or CFA that manages my business monthly.

Y N   I have an accountant, CPA or CFA advises me about my business.

Y N   I have sought the advice of an accountant, CPA or CFA?

Y N   True? Near that tax filing deadline date, I'm confident organized and ready to file?

Y N   False? Near that tax filing deadline, I get physically stressed thinking and dreading filing taxes?

Y N   I pay quarterly estimated taxes to offset paying at the end of the year?

Y N   These questions sound expensive but I can't afford not to do the things to make my business easier.

Now that wasn't so bad ... the second time around. Or was it? Remember, "Today is the first day of the rest of your life"? We hope you've decided to turn it all around or keep heading in the successful direction you are going.

✸ Ms. Stella's personal experience: *Once I completed my 1ˢᵗ Self Evaluation and went over it with my manager, I was pleasantly surprised to have my manager start to divulge ways he was challenging himself to improve. He shared personal goals and asked for my goals with the company. It completely refocused the way I had come to view my future and my career. I remember sitting there with dread at having to tell the manager I needed to improve. All night long I had prepared diplomatic ways to cover my faults and shortcomings. I was waiting to be scolded for my needing to improve my time management and follow-up. Instead we focused on the future and I felt free and liberated. AND grateful. As a result, I began to self-correct my bad habits and identify ways I could improve because my focus was on my future. Not my mistakes. I could see the possibility because it was the same track the manager had taken. I went on to achieve my goal of Store Manager with another company. I always gave my assistants and employees the opportunity to evaluate themselves with a successful result. I encouraged them to dream and got them to see how far they could go in a future with good habits.*

As you've taken this Pop Quiz for the 2nd time, focus on your future and identify the bad habits you'll have to leave behind. You can't take them into a successful future, leave them in the past.

☝**Quote: Nathaniel Baker, Sr., Beauty Supply Salesman**

I visited the salons Mrs. Carver-Goldring worked in, managed, and owned since 1977. As a beauty supply salesman, I observed Mrs. Carver-Goldring's professional treatments to her customers, co-workers, and staff members. She has developed professional skills by going on our company sponsored trips to management classes, hair styling workshops, hair, and beauty shows.

Mrs. Carver-Goldring has made a conscious decision to follow her dream and to share her experiences and knowledge with the world through writing her book. I am endorsing Mrs. Mary Carver Goldring as an author of a book to help hair stylists to understand what is required and expected of them to work in, to manager, or to own a successful beauty salon.

Thoughts/Ideas: _____

_____

_____

_____

_____

_____

_____

_____

_____

_____

_____

_____

_____

_____

_____

_____

_____

_____

_____

_____

_____

_____

_____

_____

_____

_____

_____

_____

_____

_____

_____

_____

The After Self-Evaluation and Self-Correction Summary Sheet

BE Honest, BE Brave and BE Courageous!

1. Professionalism 6 questions .... How many Yes? _____ How many No? _____
How and what can I improve: _____

_____

_____

What am I doing right: _____
What I can change easily: _____

2. Marketing/Advertisement 9 questions ...... How many Yes? _____ How many No? _____
How and what can I improve: _____

_____

_____

What am I doing right: _____
What I can change easily: _____

3. Time 5 questions .... How many Yes? _____ How many No? _____
How and what can I improve: _____

_____

_____

What am I doing right: _____
What I can change easily: _____

4. Knowledge 5 questions .... How many Yes? _____ How many No? _____

How and what can I improve: _____

_____

_____

What am I doing right: _____

What I can change easily: _____

5. Skill & Technique 6 questions .... How many Yes?
_____ How many No? _____

How and what can I improve: _____

_____

_____

What am I doing right: _____

What I can change easily: _____

6. Continued Education 4 questions .... How many Yes?
_____ How many No? _____

How and what can I improve: _____

_____

_____

What am I doing right: _____

What I can change easily: _____

7. Personal & Service 12 questions .... How many Yes?
_____ How many No? _____

How and what can I improve: _____

_____

_____

What am I doing right: _____

What I can change easily: _____

8. Business 7 questions .... How many Yes?
_____ How many No? _____

How and what can I improve: _____

_____

_____

What am I doing right: _____

What I can change easily: _____

Talley your honest answers to the 54 Self-Evaluation questions.

Total Yes Answers_____ Total NO Answers _____

A+ 51-52 A 48-50 B 44-47 C39-43 D 30-38 F-29 OR BELOW

75% (40) OF MY 54 ANSWERS WERE NO! (NO'S ARE NOT SO GOOD)

T F   I know I need to change but I don't know where to begin.

T F   I'm failing in my career, I've been thinking about a career change but I love this one.

T F   I don't think I'm the problem, the economy is bad, it's the salon owners fault but it's not my fault.

T F   I have bad adult habits that need to be improved, I lack motivation to improve.

T F   I'm not smart enough to improve, I lack focus.

T F   This profession is not a lucrative career for anyone except celebrity beauty service professionals.

The problem/excuse is: _____

_____

What I can change easily: _____

75% (40) of my 54 Answers were YES!
(Yes's are good)

T F   I've always been a type A, do my best, improve where I can, self-correct type of person.

T F   I've had a great mentor or coach in the profession that has guided my career.

T F   I read self help books to stay motivated and focused. Failure is not an option for me.

T F   I'm planning to take my career to the next level, learn more techniques and ask for more money.

T F   There is room for improvement in the _____ area, I was surprised or not by that.

What I'm doing right: _____

Where there's room for improvement: _____

It's time to ...
Change For the
Good, Better, Best!

"A Bad Attitude is like a flat tire,
You can't go anywhere until
you change it"

⏳ Getting Ready To Change
... For the Better

Most people underestimate the time and energy it takes to achieve anything of lasting value in their lives. Have you heard that saying, "If it was that easy, everyone would be doing it?' With that being said, don't worry because you are in good shape now that you've read the 10 keys and have taken your pop quiz. The first part of fixing a problem is the dreaded diagnosis, right. You go to the Doctor if you're sick, he figures out what's wrong and gives you a prescription. Your pipe burst under your sink, you shut the water off, figure out what's wrong, drive to Home Depot or call a plumber.

What is wrong with your business? What is the Diagnosis, do you need to call in a professional or can you diagnose, treat and cure the problem. There may or may not be a hefty financial bill attached to this diagnosis. Some folks may need just a little sweat equity. How much sweat, well that is all up to you?

By now, you've uncovered some areas of your business attitude, habits and outlook that may need some tweaking, some minor adjusting or a complete overhaul. You realize you need to change some things if you want to seek more business success in your life. If you've been a student of motivation and self help booklets the following information is not new for you. It will just be a reminder or refresher course. However if you've never taken a self-motivation or self-help class or watched anything on TV about changing for the better you may need to read this guide booklet twice and REALIZE, oh this does apply to ME. NOT just ALL my co-workers and friends I know in the industry.

If you are honest with yourself, just admit it. You have not really tried everything and nothing worked! STOP telling yourself that lie. You may have dibble-dabbled in a few solutions, bought some marketing products (business cards still in the box with the wrong phone number or address on them). You may have read the first couple of pages of a motivational book or magazine article, but you haven't given any solution a full honest thorough complete try.

When we, me and you? When WE are in denial about how bad our situation is, we tend to avoid positive conversations, positive people and positive situations because that means admitting to ourselves that we are the problem. We tend to gossip about others, ask and start negative conversations about other's to deflect attention on ourselves when we feel pitiful, defeated, depressed and confused. These symptoms and actions are a real indication that it's time to admit to ourselves we need to change. It is actually painful to hear this and know it's true.

Another indicator is jealousy or envy when it's painful to hear how well someone else is doing, or see your colleagues, co-workers and friends succeeding or at least looking successful. But don't worry about that because you just never know for sure if anyone is really succeeding, so don't be envious. Trust what you are reading, when you are failing miserably at your business and you don't have a readily available solution to fix the problems, you could actually go into a functional depression just thinking about it and then the worse thing will happen. You find any negative outlook, person, and/or habit to compound your belief that you are a failure and pretty satisfied to do nothing about it but complain. WOW, if that sounds familiar you've come to the right

GB-guide booklet. Have you ever seen Stevie Wonder walk on stage alone? No he needs someone to guide him, then he sits down to play beautiful music. Allow this booklet to be your guide.

Trust that other's know you need to change, but when you are the one who may realize you need to change the motivation can be like a slow leak in a tire, you've gone flat. You've tossed the notion of change to the side and opted for the lazy, "I'm doing alright" attitude. The old, "I know what works but I don't feel like putting the energy into it right now."

No matter who you are or what stage of life you find yourself, you can change right now. In this moment you can change your attitude to the "I'm gonna be the HERO or SHERO in my very own life"! As you read the following Cycle of emotions reflect on where you might be or have been in the past. Decide to gather up the necessary energy and "GROW THROUGH" each step it will take to begin to change for the better. Grow through is another way of saying "Go through." In life you will go through so many different experiences. If you choose to learn from them and become better, stronger, healthier then you ... "Grow Through." If those negative experiences have made you bitter, pessimistic, doubtful of yourself and others than you will plain and simply keep on "Going through." So *choose* to "GROW THROUGH."

Thoughts/Ideas: _____

_____

_____

_____

_____

_____

_____

_____

The Very Surprising Quick Stages of Emotion during a change for the better.

These steps are really *quick stages of emotions* you can expect to *"go through"* when taking on any new venture, changing for the better, or doing things differently. If you make it to step 5 then you are *"growing through."* You can go through all 5 steps in 1 day or over a week or a two week time period. For instance, you could get the guide book in hand and on the way home start to feel any one of steps 2 through 4. As you look over at the booklet on the car seat or while in the passenger seat you decided to thumb through it and the fear, doubt, worry and concern creep in ever so sternly rising up from your brain matter. You could walk into your business establishment or home and stuff this booklet as far down into your bag or the back of the cabinet as humanly possible. Oh you'll make sure not to leave a tip peeking its positive little head out to make you feel guilty. It's human nature to want to stay right where we are. It's comfortable and familiar territory. When you feel these varied emotions picture us, your authors of this GB smiling saying, "I told you so, but you can GROW through these steps"

IF you've purchased this guide booklet at one of the "How to get and keep seminars," we hope you left the class excited and motivated. You should be fully immersed in the emotions of step 1 below. If you've purchased the guide booklet and you've gotten through to this point, keep reading and get ready to ride the roller coaster of success.

The Emotional "**Roller Coaster**" of Change

1st Emotion: Joy, happiness, excitement and enthusiasm.

"Yeah Me!"

Roller Coaster Ride: Get ready for the chain link climb of Anticipation ...

You feel like, I have a solution, a direction, goals, some motivation for my future! When you decide to change you feel relieved that the future will look different, brighter, and happier than the past. You **know** that you'll be able to pay your bills on time with all the money you'll make. You **feel,** that for the first time in a long time you'll love yourself and have more self respect. You **want** to take your life and business to the next level.

Well hold on to that feeling because success lies in forming good habits. Successful people do things that people who fail don't want to do. The secret to breakthroughs is "*follow-through.*"

☺ **Step 1 Emotion discover, "What's going on with me":** So, you have decided you're going to clean your work area. Or you're determined to set your alarm for 2 hours early and not hit the snooze button. Perhaps you scheduled clients so that you can send your "We've missed you" postcards during your lunch break. You are excited and want to get started on the right track. Take note ... It's easy to overcrowd that to do list when we're excited. You get overwhelmed and can't figure out where the excitement went.

When the excitement starts to wear off ... Grow through it: Remember that new car smell always wears off eventually. Try these quick pick me ups in small stages, don't try to do too much: 1. Clean up, because clean neat surroundings inspire. 2. Self-compliments look in the mirror and say; keep up the good work with a smile. 3. Pat yourself on the back for each and every effort you are making. 4. Giving compliments and encouraging words to others will inspire them to encourage you as well. These are all ways to keep your excitement and enthusiasm up. Make sure to surround yourself with a positive partner who is already where you want to be. You might have to stop listening or spending so much *success bashing good times* with your friend who's a Debbie Downer or Neville the Negative. Ditch'em! Or at least cut them back some, get them out of your ear. See you-wouldn't want to be you. Watch out, you just may become Suzy Success, their inspiration. Keep moving forward.

2nd Emotion: Frustration, Concern, Shock and Doubt

"What have I gotten myself into"

Roller Coaster Ride: Picture your face when going down that first hill ...

It's amazing how quickly the excitement of a new challenge can change to that dreaded feeling of "Who did I think I was trying to become." That's because when you begin to change for the better you start to uncover obstacles. Your old habits like a rubber band fight to come swinging back with a vengeance pretty quickly.

Not to mention, the folks you told when you were excited are watching. The average people in your life may not be responding in the way you had hoped. They are not as excited for you as you'd hoped. Questions cloud your mind, like what am I supposed to be doing? Why did I think this would be so easy? You look in the mirror and ask, why wasn't I just born a Rockefeller or Oprah's cousin!

☺ Step 2 Emotion discover, "What's Going On with me": As a result of my marketing, so many clients are calling me and I'm not used to working this hard, coming in this early or staying this late. I've gotten 10 message responses to the post cards and I feel guilty that I haven't called them back. Or perhaps you've only gotten 2 responses to the post cards and you feel discouraged. Is it because you haven't made time to make the follow up calls? You've hit the snooze button four times instead of twice in the effort to get to work early before your clients. The effort you are making is harder than you'd thought it would be and the benefits aren't happening as fast as you thought they would. The key here is to follow the emotional trail, identify the emotion and be honest about why you are feeling this way. Good, bad or indifferent.

When you start to feel frustration and fear, don't freak out ... Grow through it: Breath. Calm down. Be grateful Believe it or not, this is the point many people turn back. STEP 2, can you believe it? This is just the 2nd step. Step 2 and already giving up? Wow, scream to yourself to keep on moving forward. Tell yourself that "You can do it!" Tell yourself, "I deserve this change for the better." Right now, say it aloud: "I DESERVE TO CHANGE FOR THE BETTER." See yourself opening a gift, a beautifully wrapped package. Oh, what is it? Success so bright it's like looking at the sun! You cared enough to give yourself that gift? Wow you are awesome. Keep moving forward.

3rd Emotion: Denial & Fear

F.E.A.R-False Evidence Appearing Real

Roller Coaster Ride: Curves, small hills, jerking turns, it's almost over …

People always make things look so easy to get you to buy something. I knew this wouldn't work. Right now Suzy Success wants to stop reading this guide booklet. You start to avoid going on the Salon Affairs website for new inspiration. Have you started to avoid all the folks you made commitments and promises to yet? You may find yourself procrastinating again, falling into old habits; avoiding eye contact with your clients. Sleeping, eating, cooking and eating too much. AGAIN! Here come the excuses and blame. (1) I blame the co-worker who suggested this guide book. (2) I hate getting on that computer. (3) I'm out of stamps again, sending these post cards is expensive (4) My kids are too young and they need me more, my husband needs me more (5) I can't do this, it's just way too much (6) I'm not organized.

Step 3 Emotion discover, "What's Going On with me": Do you feel like giving up? Perhaps you and your AP-success partner are avoiding each other. In an effort to stop thinking or working toward your business success perhaps you have taken on more projects elsewhere. Did you throw the post cards to the back of your desk drawer yet? Where is your index card box? Are you playing Candy Crush Saga or Angry Birds on the lap top instead of putting in your client's information?

No … … … … …! When you start to sink back into the quicksand of the past … Grow through it: Yell NO, I will not step in that quick sand, I will go around it! Clean up your work station. Put on some upbeat music and get moving. Go in the bathroom and stretch, do a few jumping jacks and run in place. Look in the mirror and say: "I DESERVE TO CHANGE FOR THE BETTER" Go and send your new clients a "Welcome to the Salon/Spa/Barber Shop card." At the same time send your referring clients a "Thank you for the Referral" card. Kiss and Bless the Postcards put them in the outgoing mail or drop them in the mail box on the way home. Keep the success train moving forward, toot toot.

4th Emotion: Depression, Anger, Quitting

"WHY ME, I QUIT!"

Roller Coaster Ride: I didn't get on the Coaster, my friends rode without me ...

Most often Depression, Anger and deciding to quit are the three fingers that are pointing back at us when we are pointing one finger at someone else. Do it now! Point that one finger. See those three fingers pointing back at you beginning from the bottom with the pinky finger? What are some of the excuses you are telling yourself? Do you even like you? Do you think you are smart? Do you think you are destined for failure, because you are a woman, high school or college dropout, a man in a typical women's industry, disabled, blind, have one limb, are of a particular ethnicity or sexual orientation?

Step 4 Emotion discover, "What's Going On with me": I never wanted to be a millionaire! Why did I buy this booklet? Why did I attend that class? Why do I even try, for real? I'm glad I bought the book. I'm glad the tools are working. But? But what! I just feel. I just feel what? Come on pull it together and think of the reasons you want to succeed. The reasons you don't want to feel Depressed anymore. The reason Anger is attacking more than your outlook on life, it's making you sick. Quit? No way not you, do not quit. Do not give up on you.

If you get mad! Angry! Depressed! Grow through it: Success is ultimately up to us. Change is up to us. We have to give ourselves that gift of changing for the better. It is important to believe in ourselves. But if you know that you don't feel or believe you can do it, start by saying some nice things about yourself to yourself. Like for instance, "I want to do this!" "I need to do this!" "I will give myself this gift!" But even more importantly, **DO! Keep Moving** forward. **Move! Do! Start moving forward!** Use the tools and skills that we are giving you; put them into practice everyday and you will get positive results. Even if you are mad at where you are right now in your life, you can change it and that is something to get excited about … which if you remember is step 1.

5th Emotion: Recommit; make a Pledge & Promise to myself

"I will reach my goals." "I believe in my ability to move my life forward."

Roller Coaster Ride: I made it off alive, I'm glad I did it and proud of me …

Oh now here comes the fun part! Remembering and getting excited about the future. What is better than feeling excitement and joy, being happy, secure and free? Maybe, making a plan and working that plan and enjoying the success of your labor for a start! When you sit down and look at your appointments for the day and realize you barley have a lunch break smile, don't get frustrated. Add up the potential tickets for the day and remember to pay yourself first. Put that $10 a day x 52 weeks in a year=$2,600 in that travel to Europe fund. Holla!

Step 5 Emotion discover, "What's Going On with me": Whew! Yeah baby, I like this feeling. Success as I define it. I've made some changes and I'm so happy with the outcome. My clients seem to be happier too. They respect me, I respect myself. My long-time client even referred her best friend and a few church members too. All because I asked, I can hardly believe I didn't ask before. All because she was excited to receive that post card in her email box. Wow, this marketing really works.

Renew your excitement! Grow through it! Just do it ... Renew your excitement for the career that you've chosen? The Beauty Service Industry is fun! It's a dream career when you are making money and successfully servicing your clients with professionalism. Remind yourself of all the wonderful reasons it's an awesome and challenging career. **Add some of your own reasons to the list below** and keep moving forward with excitement and joy at going to school, passing the state board exam and getting your license. Then carving out a path and choosing such a fabulous career.

1. I play a special role in the special occasions of my client's lives.
2. I help my clients relieve their stress in a very stressful world.
3. I make life easier for my clients, doing for them what they could possibly do for themselves. But they choose to pay me to do it for them.
4. I work close to home, set my own hours, set and reach goals for how much money I want to make.
5. _____
6. _____
7. _____
8. _____

9. _____
10. _____

Get on that train to success as you define it!

Who is in your head thinking for you? Did you know your thoughts are controlling your actions? Your words are controlling your thoughts. Who is responsible for change in your life?

There was an email I received years ago that read, a young boy and his father walked through the forest and the young boy fell almost drawing blood from his knee. Crying out he yelled, "Ouch." Suddenly a voice yelled back, "Ouch." "Who is that," the boy yelled? That mysterious voice yelled back, "Who is that." The boy stood up defiantly and yelled, "Come forward you coward." "Come forward you coward," came the voice just as strong. "Stop mocking me, I hate you." "Stop mocking me, echoed before he could finish screaming, "I hate you." The boy became frustrated and asked his father what is going on who is that? The father yelled, "I love you." "I love you" came the voice reply. "You are smart, intelligent and very good looking," the father yelled. As the voice echoed the father's sentiment exactly, "You are smart, intelligent and very good looking." The young boy was amazed. The father looked at his young son who began to smile a little as he stood up and brushed himself off. The father explained that what they were hearing was an echo.

Life is a lot like that echo whatever we put out into the universe for ourselves and other's comes right back to us quicker than we could ever imagine.

Going the Extra Mile

Paying the Price for lasting success.

The scoring in archery is sin.

If you don't reach your target after reading this GB and applying the techniques, it is a sin.

Now that you've got the keys, it's time to soar.

Going the Extra Mile

Paying the Price for lasting success.

Once you focus on making the basic 10 keys daily professional habits, it's time to unlock the understanding and acceptance that "I will have to change some bad habits" and/or "I'm proud of the good habits that have gotten me this far"! Unlock your potential with your new keys. It's that simple. Be the Hero or Shero in your very own life. Remember you are the star of YOUR very own reality show!

The goal of the 10 Keys is to have you complete the Pop Quiz first. Then read the 10 Keys and rank each one according to what you need to work on the most. Then with keys in hand begin with that first step, just like a new born baby. Give yourself some loving encouragement as you grow for the changes you'll have to make to succeed.

Once you've mastered the basic 10 keys then you've decided that you want to go the extra mile with the goal of keeping the clientele you've built by mastering and owning those basic and simple ideals. You are now confident in asking your clients to refer family, friends, co-workers and strangers on the street to you. Over time you'll realize, as a BSP life will undoubtedly revolve around you somewhat. Meaning you will be on the checklist of the planning of your client's lives. There will be first dates, job interviews, weddings, baby's being born, funerals, trips to the hospital, kids' taking pictures in pre-school, prom, then going off to college. Being a trusted BSP such as a cosmetologist, esthetician, nail tech, barber, massage therapist, makeup artist, etc is a very personal experience in people's lives. "WE ARE IMPORTANT IN THE LIVES OF OUR CLIENTS." Treasure and have fun with that very important fact. Get a few photo albums and fill them with the pictures people give you, make sure they sign the back and give them rock star status.

As BSP's we touch more than just heads, feet, faces and bodies, we touch hearts. We aid in giving self-esteem, confidence, comfort, relaxation in a stressful world. This is why we walk the fine line of being professional and getting too personal. Keep your outlook and client relationship professional. Your clients shouldn't know all your trials and tribulations, bad news and ups and downs. That information is for your friends and family. The exception is that if someone close to you passed away or you have to have surgery your clients may want to know so they can give you a sympathy card or a get well card. The rule is they may not want to hear about each new love interest or your financial troubles, your differences with your children. Even if they are telling you all about their life dilemmas make it a point to listen and sympathize. The reason is you just never know what your clients are thinking about having to listen to your melodrama. Is it worth the risk that they begin to see you as a knucklehead person who makes bad life choices and question why they would trust you with their business?

EXTRA MILE TARGET NO. 1

Take note of special occasions and milestones in the lives of your clients.

Because … It is a privilege and an honor knowing that our clients are most surely including us, their BSP in celebrations of their Birthdays, Weddings and Anniversaries or that Congratulation Celebration with a facial, massage or a new hair style. These milestones are so important in the lives of our clients from planning to execution, don't forget to send or hand them a card to show them that you remember and celebrate with them. Also if they are planning surgery, stressed or grieving we'll play apart in that as well so a get well, sympathy or thinking of you card would be appropriate. Also don't forget those thank you cards for gifts they give you or periodically sending them a card for their continued and loyal patronage of your services.

Keep it simple, make a Card Catalog in a portable file sorter with cards for all occasions. It is awesome if you are organized enough to mail the cards in a timely manner. If not just give it to them at the end of their appointment. To get organized pay attention and include special occasion with a chime on your cell phone or tablet's alarm reminder. You can easily place all the birthdays on the calendar once you take it off their initial Consultation Sheets. Keep track of the day they first chose you as their BSP with a yearly Anniversary card. If a client mentions they are going to be in the hospital consult with them about a care free hair style for surgery with no hair pins or make sure they get that pedicure, massage or facial before they are unable to seek your professional services for weeks after surgery.

Also make sure to have several photo albums to keep the pictures your clients give you. You could title each album weddings, graduations, special occasions etc. Or you could simply keep an album a year.

Type or write something on the inside that says, Live, Love & Laugh or Life is worth celebrating making sure to write your Salon name inside as well. Remembering your clients is a great way to make sure they know they are appreciated.

 ## EXTRA MILE TARGET NO. 2

Make Brief Professional Phone Calls.

Because … The sound of your voice on the phone makes a professional connection that money can't buy. You have undoubtedly been at home cooking dinner and had a telemarketer machine call you. Or perhaps you've had those campaign volunteers call you repeatedly. Why do they call you? Because making that human connection by phone works. It can be a little irritating at times when you feel like you've been solicited. But when you hear a friendly familiar voice it can be a wonderful surprise.

Why not use the phone as your professional tool for your business. Making a brief phone call when one of your regular clients hasn't scheduled an appointment in three or four weeks could be just what the client needed. Perhaps they'd gotten too busy to call you, they'll be glad to hear from you in that case. Or it could become a fact finding mission for you, maybe they'll tell you something over the phone that they were too uncomfortable to tell you in person such as the last massage was too rough, the facial irritated their skin, or the hairstyle didn't last overnight. If your client tells you something like that, **don't start making excuses**. Be ready to ask for a chance to improve. Don't corner them and make them feel bad for not telling you sooner, be glad that you've found out and be ready to make it right. Perhaps they are laid off work or have a financial strain. Send them a coupon or offer $10 off a service.

A phone call when your client is at home seriously ill or in the hospital takes a moment but the sentiment will last much longer. Keep the phone call brief by stating, I'm simply calling to make sure you are doing well after surgery or to see if you have gotten over your cold. Ask non personal questions like, how is physical therapy going. I'm sorry to hear that the recovery is taking longer than expected or I'm glad to hear you're feeling much better is an appropriate response.

Don't ask if there is anything you can do if you are not prepared to do anything they ask. Instead if you are willing to make a paid house call, suggest or ask is that needed saying, "our house call fee is $_____ . I could see you Thursday morning at 9 if that is convenient. If they take you up on a house call, give yourself plenty of time to set up, break down and get back to your business establishment when scheduling that appointment house call. If you can send a carry out meal or flowers, something specific for long time loyal clients inquire about someone being at home to receive it. Drop off a case of water or order pizza for the clients children. Those sentiments can be written off in most cases as a business expense. Talk to your tax professional about the specifics.

To end the call, simply state the truth. I just wanted to give you a brief call and let you know of my concern. Please continue to get better and I will see you soon.

 ## Extra Mile Target No. 3

Be a good listener and not so much of a talker.

Because … Clients come to the BSE for more than just their scheduled appointment service. They could be coming to relax and don't want to talk or listen. They could also be coming and can't wait to blow off steam about their day. Be in-tuned to your client's moods. Most important, the initial connection should be about business, be a good listener to your client's desires for their current appointment. Always remember you are in business. Be prepared to help them decide on new services or add on services they could benefit from. If they express changing or updating their service be knowledgeable about what services you offer to meet your client's needs. Second, be aware if they are in the mood to talk or if they simply want silence during their appointment. If they are in the mood to talk **let them talk** and practice becoming a good listener. Keeping your personal opinions to yourself is a wise and professional decision. If they ask for your opinion about a personal matter, turn it back on the client by asking them, "What do you think you should do?" Or ask the client, "Have you thought of a solution that could work best for you?" If you have a similar relevant experience you may want to briefly share it focusing on why it worked for you. Above all be positive in your conversation and remember that you are not your client's personal therapist. Keep strong opinions about your client's personal life to yourself. Above all, keep your personal problems to yourself. Share your problems, cares and concerns with your friends or family members, not your clients. Even though our clients seem like good friends, they are truly paying clients. Keep it professional so you won't live to regret.

Remember also not to pry or be noisy. Let your clients tell you what they want you to know about themselves and IF they tell you something, keep it in the strictest confidence. Remember as clients refer people to you, you've undoubtedly forgotten who referred whom and who knows whom. You could end up telling the co-worker, relative or best friend something about a person who asked you to keep their confidence. Even if you don't repeat a name, a story could be familiar to your client and they could figure it all out. Gossip is the worst threat to true professional service. If you must gossip, make it celebrity gossip and let your client do most of the talking.

 EXTRA MILE TARGET NO. 4

Ask about friends, relatives, family members to extend your service.

Because … this is the best way to build your customer base by reminding your current clients that you could be servicing other people they know. Once you've come to know your client, extend your service by asking about the needs of your client's family and friends. For instance, ask about the condition of your client's daughter's hair and nails. Even a son and husband need some type of service. Ask, have they got a stressed out boss or co-worker that could use a deep tissue massage? Suggest and remind clients of gift certificates and retail products that may benefit the client's extended family. ASK for clients. Give clients business cards and ask them to give the cards to co-workers, family or friends.

🟐 *Stella's Personal Experience: As a nail tech, once I had a client let me know that her husband's toenail had cut her in the middle of the night. She thought it was a thumb tack or something in their bed until she looked down at his bloody big toenail the next morning. She asked if I serviced men. Of course, I told her. She stated she'd never seen any men in the salon and that her husband may be uncomfortable there. He's not a salon type of man, she told me. He doesn't even like to come in if he has to bring me. I was glad that my nail station was in a more private area in the back of the salon. I assured her I'd take care of making him feel comfortable and I helped her make an early morning appointment when the salon was not as busy. I made sure to have male reading material on hand for him as well. I prominently displayed the male scented lotions he could choose from and as a result I gained a faithful* client. I also began asking my clients to have their husbands come in for a pedicure and manicure and gained several new clients. I took the time to make my area more neutral and male friendly too.

As a result of the above experience I questioned myself, were there any other areas of revenue I was overlooking. I had male prices on my brochure, but that was obviously overlooked by some of my female clients. I can honestly say 90% of my male clients were referred by females. I began verbally suggesting (pushing) gift certificates during May and June for father's day and graduations. I listened intensely for people stuck with that "what to give _____ as a gift?" A paraffin pedicure I would suggest, it will make your recipient feel so special. I increased my gift certificate revenue and gained new clients.

✹ *Stella's Personal Experience: During this time of reaching out to female clients asking for male client referrals, one of my female clients suggested that she'd never have her husband come to the salon because she felt the women would flirt with him. "He's very ticklish too," she told me as she glanced at my cleavage. I hadn't noticed my cleavage but I became well aware of it that day and tied my apron higher around my neck. I took that comment very seriously. It's easy to have a quick emotional opinion of someone's comment. But just realize as a professional that what one client shares is always what others are thinking. When you feel a rush of negative emotions from a client's personal opinion, stop and ask yourself why you feel so strongly about it. My first gut reaction was that the client was very insecure. But you never know what had happened in her life or experiences that warranted the comment. I also felt honored that she could share her thoughts with me, I then chose to use the comment to learn and correct my behavior to my benefit. That moment was a huge eye opener for me to have these women trust me to service their husbands. As a professional, I took the extra initiative to wear a smock more often when servicing men and if it was an extremely hot Apron wearing day I'd pull my apron up over my cleavage. Going so far to bend over in the mirror to see if anything was showing.*

In all honesty I noticed that the pedicure and touch can be very sensual. People respond in different ways and some are very ticklish. I've practiced making my strokes strong and determined as not to evoke inappropriate responses. Some of the men moaned in pleasure when those feet hit hot water and as I massaged their feet and calves. I make sure not to look at their faces to acknowledge it. They became very comfortable in my chair over time and I never take it for granted that I have the trust of their wives and girlfriends who are my long time clients. I always try to keep it professional and drama free.

 ## EXTRA MILE TARGET NO. 5

Make note of area convenience and amenities for clients

Because … Clients appreciate any gesture that makes their lives easier. Put together a list of restaurants, banks and other area convenience for clients. If you're in a strip mall, make sure to have advertisement of stores, hours and information available for your clients when they ask. Keep local bus schedules, cab and public transportation information available for clients as well. Not all clients have smart phones with internet access. Remember that not all clients are savvy at using the new technology that exists.

 ## EXTRA MILE TARGET NO. 6

Get in on the Holiday Spirit and make your clients feel special

Because, it makes people feel special and they remember how you made them feel. On Holiday's or the day before if you are working and you celebrate the holiday get in the spirit. Give chocolate, roses or carnations to your clients on Valentines Day and Mother's day weekend. There are countless catalogs that offer bulk gifts relevant to each holiday for clients. When giving a gift make sure to somehow attach your business card, slogan or contact information with a "thank you for your continued patronage" note. A gift is a thank you, if you don't attach a card make sure to stop your client, look them in the eye and say, "I appreciate your continued patronage." Then present the gift being clear that it is a reward of appreciation. Make sure at the end of the year to give your clients a personalized thank you gift that doubles as an advertisement and appreciation for their continued patronage. Calendars, ink pens, picture magnets, canvas totes are great end of year gifts that advertise your service.

 ## EXTRA MILE TARGET NO. 7

Make it a habit to teach and learn from other staff members

Why? Because having an attitude that you can't share what you know because perhaps other stylist might take your clients is a fear that may affect your professional relationships. Clients can feel the competitive, fearful and uptight atmosphere of a BSE. Always think of the people you work with as fellow professional. You'll often seem and spend more time with them than some family members. So be nice, cordial and professional. This will eliminate the disease of stress related illness from your body. Make it a choice to enjoy going to work, be a part of solutions, not a constant part of problems at the BSE.

Trust and believe that there are enough clients to go around to all willing Beauty Service Professionals. Don't live in fear that someone is going to steal your clients. Everyone does something well and better than most, we can all learn, grow and improve from each other's experience. It helps to compliment other co-workers when you see them perfecting a technique or doing something well. Remember to share knowledge and be helpful so that when it comes time to learn, you want hesitate to ask for help.

☝**Quote:** Gloria Brown, Retired Cosmetologist.

I began my Cosmetology career because I love working with people and helping them. My client's children grew up in my chair and clients followed me from salon to salon. I personally had never met a fellow stylist, owner who was as helpful as Ms. Mary's daughter Deborah Collins. I worked at Deborah's salon Family Affair II and that's how I met her mother and Sister Ms. Mary & Stella when they closed Family Affair I and came to work with Deborah. I had been in the business over 35 years when I met their family, they were the best family you could ever meet. All of them gave you a helping hand in everything. Ms. Mary showed me styles that I couldn't do. Even though she was older than I am, she taught me how to keep the younger generation of clients happy. She also put me on the right track with my health. She is an Angel that keeps everybody on the right track.

 ## EXTRA MILE TARGET NO. 8

Take time and learn to truly care about your clients.

Why? Because people know when you care, they feel it. Have you heard the quote, "People will forget your name, they may forget what you did, but they will never forget how you made them feel." When you care, you'll do your best. You'll remember little things clients tell you in confidence and you'll remember to ask them about it. If you are a great listener clients will share concerns because in your caring hands they are relaxed. This is a quote from one of my clients on the occasion of my 70th birthday. She wrote this letter and framed it and it really touched me because this is truly how I want my clients to feel.

👍**Quote:** Mrs. Mary Reid, Client for over 35 years.

"Mrs. Mary Carver Goldring: I love you very much and you are one of the best friends I have ever had. You give generously from your heart and feed me spiritually. God was in the front and healthy was next. I followed you to every Salon God sent you to. I came to be with you 35 years ago. No one can sit under your hair care and not feel the real person you are. You are a virtuous woman with a loving & caring family. You are special to my entire family. May God our Father continue to bless you daily and abundantly in the name of the Jesus. God gives for a season: thank you for my season. You are never far from my heart. God told us to love one another as He has loved us. Stay the great lady that you are and never change. You have always been a breath of fresh air—again I thank you and always keep God before you and His love in your heart. Remember this to sit in Mary's chair is not just about hair. If you are sick-physician comes out. Problems in your life-counselor comes out. Feeling low-out comes the minister. Need a word-out comes the teacher. When you leave and on your way home, you think "wow she just made my day." Hey Lady T-Happy Birthday and many more- God Bless you, you have been chosen His Spirit is upon you.

Thoughts/Ideas: _____
_____
_____
_____
_____
_____

Sail into your future

My
Professional Vision
&
Goals for
My
Future

My Professional Vision & Goals for My Future

The life you lead right now can change if you want it to. How, you ask? First envision this new life and then create a plan of action for the changes. Next be focused on the steps it will take to make the changes happen that you've designed in your plan. Just be convinced as you look back that where you are in life right now is happening as a result of your past decisions and your actions. Your life will not change arbitrarily for the better unless you have a firm fixed vision of how you want your life to look in your mind. Planning and Action should be your two new favorite words. When a builder wants to build a house, it starts in the mind, they design plans and they build it. Right?

It's no joke that a dream can become reality. Faith (believing in what you don't yet see) is real. It has been proven scientifically in recent years that prayer (asking with positive belief in what you are asking for) is real. How do you want your future to look? Do you want your future to be different from your past, the same or worse? Right now, are you simply drifting like a little lake boat with no ores? Taking what comes, blowing and heading any way the wind blows you? Are you hoping for your life to get better or be different but not **planning** or taking any planned **action** for it to change? If you don't' know what, how, who or when, try this exercise.

After you read this dream exercise, sit back, relax and close your eyes. Picture with reckless abandon your ideal 24 hour day. Start from the moment you wake up; was your bedroom clean, beautiful and comfortable? How are your children behaving, is their homework neat and complete as they leave for school? Do you eat breakfast with your family together, or drive through McDonalds? What is your husband doing? What kind of car do you drive to work or are you chauffeured to work? When you walk in to your work environment how does it look? Slowly peruse the establishment, is the supply closet full of supplies, are the towels clean, is the floor waxed and shinny, trash cans empty? Is your work day full of clients, picture them leaving happy with your service. How much money did you make? Count it up, look at all those checks and wow the receipt from the debit machine looks like your Christmas list to Santa. End with you closing the door as you leave the business, was it modern with technology every where, sleek and white or red and gaudy or neutral and modern? When you get home, do you watch the sunset from the beech house deck or see the city lights from the sky scraper terrace. What do you do before closing your eyes to sleep? Just think about this for a moment, whatever your dream is there is someone living a life almost identical to the one you just dreamt. It's not impossible to achieve your ideal. You just have to have an idea of your ideal lifestyle to begin living it.

Now go, close your eyes and dream big! Once you've got it firmly fixed in your mind, describe it by writing it down on a clean sheet of paper. Sketch out the business establishment. How much does the house and the car cost that you envisioned? Google it and add the price to the page. How much are the houses in that neighborhood you dreamt? Now honestly answer these questions in the dream questionnaire.

Dream Exercise Questionnaire

1. (1a)Could this be my reality? ____Yes ____No ____Maybe ____
   I don't know where to begin to make it happen. (1b)I'm living
   this reality ready to take it to the next level. ____yes ____not yet
   ____no-way close (1c)Why, how or why not? _____

   _____

   _____

2. Did the dream exercise seem like a joke or where you surprised
   to look behind your own eyeballs to the fantasy that lay there?
   Have you thought of it many times before satisfied that you have
   this dream, but never imagining any of it could be true? Are you
   officially on your way there, or have no doubt that what you
   dreamt could be a reality? Perhaps the dream wasn't far from
   your reality. The question to answer here is: (2a) When you think
   of the dream, how does it make you feel? Happy, excited, sad,
   frightened, ashamed, jealous, confused, doubtful, grateful what
   emotions. (2b) Why?_____

   _____

   _____

3. (3a) Do you feel this dream day is close to being a reality? (3b)
   Why, what are you doing to make it happen? (Positive Self-talk,
   Striving, Taking Business Courses, Learning from a Mentor)
   (3c) What are you doing to prevent you from living it? (Lazy,
   Stubborn, Low Self-Esteem, Negative Self-Talk)

   _____

   _____

4. (4a) Do you have goals set for this type of reality? ____Y ____N
   (4b) What are the goals you've set that would make this dream

day a reality? _____

_____

_____

5. If you answered yes to the question above, Congratulations you've set goals great! (5a)Write them here. If you answered no, use this space to write what you can change and goals that answer how can you get to where you want to be? Example (Problem: I'm Late to work 80% of time-I can wake up to inspirational music to get motivated about my day. I can only drink on the weekend so I will not be so hung over when the alarm clock goes off M-F. I can make sure my kids are trained in a routine that helps everyone in the house be in bed by 9:00)

    1. _____

    2. _____

    3. _____

6. (6a) Have you ever spoken to, read a book about or asked questions of a person who is living this dream life? ____Y ____N (6b) I don't know anyone personally. ____Y ____N (6c) I see successful people at trade shows but I have no questions ready to ask them. ____Y ____N (6d) I have talked to successful people at trade shows, I make it a point to view their website or have written or emailed them with questions. ____Y ____N (6e) I passed a dream establishment at the mall, but have never stopped in to ask the owner any questions. ____Y ____N (6f) I've called or made an appointment to ask the owner of an establishment I admire some business questions. ____Y ____N (6g) I have seen beautiful establishments in a magazine and always admire them, but I could never imagine working in a classy beautiful place like that. ____Y ____N

    I want to ask (successful person's name) or I have spoken to:

    _____

I would ask them or I did ask: _____

_____

If I ever get the chance or better yet, I will make it a point to ask the following questions of a successful BSP that I admire:

_____

_____

I will also drop them a note or make sure they know I admire and appreciate their inspiration to me.

7. (7a) Are you excited yet? ____Y ____N (7b) Do you believe in your ability, courage, determination and stamina to create a life you can be proud of? ____Y ____N

☑ Positive Affirmations

The word "Affirmation" is a positive **statement** of the truth of something. All those negative beliefs you have, you are repeating them so they are your "truth." You believe what you are saying. Below we have compiled a list of positive affirmations to replace the negative statements you may be saying to yourself. Remember our minds are our mental computers. Whatever we feed into the brain is like we are programming it. Our body will easily respond to that programming with actions. We need to change that roller coaster of negativity. Its time to get off the negative roller coaster ride and get on the Concord to your fabulous destination … Success

★Most importantly as you say the affirmation feel the words and visualize their meaning. For example when you say the word "health" see or visualize yourself healthy. When you say the statement "my Appointment book is blessed" visualize it full to overflowing with clients.

☑ Stop saying … "I'm so tired." "I'm out of shape." "I feel drained." **Instead believe it when you say:** "Thank God for health & Strength." "I am energized as I think of the possibilities waiting to be unwrapped in this day." "I feel like I could run a marathon to the drive through window of my bank and deposit all the checks I'm going to collect today." "I am healthy, wealthy and wise."

☑ Stop saying … "I don't feel like going to work." "I hate that place." "I wish I could hit the lottery and quit." **Instead believe it when you say:** "I thank God for another day above ground and that I have a skill that is in demand." "I love being creative and making people feel beautiful." "I love helping people release their stress as I massage those muscles into submission." "When I hit the lottery, I'm gonna make some improvements around here."

☑ Stop saying … "I'm catching a cold, I always get sick." "I'm just a magnet for germs"

Instead believe it when you say: "I love me and take good care of myself." "I never get sick." "Germs run when they see me coming." "I always wash my hands and make sure I take my medication as directed."

☑ Stop saying … "I'm always late, I can't help it."

Instead believe it when you say: "Being on time makes my day go so much smoother." "My client's time is just as precious to them as my time is to me." "I deserve to wake up perky, get to work on time and leave on time to enjoy my evening." "Being late starts my day off wrong, so I always strive to be on time."

☑ Stop saying … "People don't have any money that's why my Appointment Book is empty."

Instead believe it when you say: "My Appointment Book is blessed, it's overflowing I always have all the clients I need and more." "My Appointment Book is jammed, crammed full of wonderful clients happy and anticipating my services."

☑ Stop saying … "I'm too old to learn anything new."

Instead believe it when you say: "I will continue to learn something new everyday until I die." "I can't wait to practice new techniques I've learned so that I can try them and impress my clients."

☑ Stop saying … "I hate to see Ms. or Mr. _____ (feel in the blank) coming they are never satisfied." "Mr. or Ms. _____ get on my nerves, I can't please him or her."

Instead believe it when you say: "Some clients help me grow and keep me on my toes. They remind me to always be professional. Ms. _____ has such high standards, I'm honored she chose me to service her needs.

113

☑ Stop saying … I can't find anything nice to say to about my co-workers or _____.

Instead believe it when you say: "I always find something positive to compliment my family, co-workers, clients and friends on. Because when we give praises, compliments daily to our circle of folks it elevates them to being and feeling grateful."

Remember these simple gestures always make people feel better and put them in a good mood. Fully embrace and accept the compliments your clients and other's give to you. Your response to a compliment should be to simply say thank you without explaining the compliment away.

☑ Stop saying negative things about your clients that you can't say to their face, instead find ways and things to say to them that will encourage them to be better. Such as, "Thank you for being on time," "I appreciate your continued patronage," "I love the way you wear your makeup," "You always dress so classy."

NOW picture this often.

Go Be … the cheerleader in your own life.

(Picture yourself in that cheerleader uniform cheering for you when you improve for the better or try really hard to change those bad habits)

Advertising/Marketing 101

Why & How to Market and Advertise for New Clients

✋ THE "Five Finger HOOK" ... Casting the line. Picking-up New Clients

What is your *hook*? In other words, what is your pick-up line for new clients? Yes, we're referring to that "pick-up" line from the 70's bar scene. Here's a few: "Hey are you about the fall, cause you look like you could use a Spring Make-over Baby." "Wow, your ends are splitting like a high school cheerleader." "Alright now you look kind of tense, you need a really good deep tissue massage don't you."

All jokes aside you need a "Hook." This hook will give you confidence when handing out your business card to pick-up new clients. A great hook should last no longer than 2 minutes and it will: Introduce you, define what you are good at (your specialty), and peak your potential clients interest. A great hook delivered with confidence will leave the potential client actually thinking I want to give this BSP a try. Approaching a client with no HOOK might leave them looking for the nearest trash can for your business card. You must look the part when using your hook. If you are a stylist specializing in color service your own hair should be representative of your skill. If you're an Esthetician the client is going to look at your skin for that healthy glow. A confident smile bubbling up from the inside is a great way to deliver a hook.

Here is how the "Hook" really works. First you need to determine what you are really good at. Then try to summarize it up in one or two lines. Use empowering words like; expert, precision, celebrated.

Whip out that thesaurus if you need to find a great word that describes what you do. Next, think of an original catchy line or "hook." Play around with this idea and get creative. Think of what you'd like to hear from a stranger providing the service you provide. What would "hook" you?

Next practice saying it in front of a mirror, co-workers and friends. Don't practice on clients, yet. There are four simple steps to the *hook* that should be used when cold calling or passing out business cards. The way to begin the *hook* is to (1) quickly begin with a compliment. Don't wait for a response, don't ask where they bought it, just don't ask a question? (2) next, go right into the *hook*, (3) then hand the person 2 business cards. (4) Close the deal with a happy thank you, look forward to hearing from you this week. End with, "You just got a little closer to fabulous." Plant a seed of, "You'd be crazy not to call me and schedule an appointment."

The reason you don't ask a question during the hook is that the hook is meant to be spontaneous and fast. You don't want to prolong the exchange. When you ask a question you have to wait for the answer and it may be a long answer. You want to stay on the subject of getting a new client, you want results. If you ask for instance, "Where did you get that blouse?" Fifteen minutes later you are still standing there hearing about your potential new clients trip to Florida and the little shop that sells these blouses. You may even have to look at Cell phone pictures of the trip.

A common occurrence when using your hook is that the potential client could ask you a question. Such as, "my nails are splitting and thin, what can I do to make that stop?" This is when if you have a website, a blog or a Facebook page you can refer them to your frequently asked questions page. Wow look at you! If you don't have a web presence, then simply inform the potential client that you offer free consultations at your BSE. You could quickly answer if time permits. For example: Client states, "my hair is so dry and brittle." BSP response: "There are so many contributing factors to dry and brittle hair, from too much caffeine to medication from health related issues or neglected over processed hair. Let me offer you a thorough consultation at my BSE and when I finish I will give you a prescription for reversing the damage to your hair. Schedule an appointment so we can get you on the way to healthier hair." By all means BSP, be equipped and ready to deliver on any statement that you make.

You will also use your hook as a catch phrase or slogan on your business cards, your website, your blog and your Facebook page. The hook should be representative of your specialty and specifically designed to pique the interest of potential new clients. This is what you are known for. It can be broad like: Linda, "The Queen of Special Event Make-up Artistry, I make your grand entrance worth the wait! Todd, Barber to the Stars. Everyone wants to be a Star!

The following are examples for passing out business cards or meeting people you want to network with. When handing your business card to anyone for any reason, use your hook. Just remember when you see a potential client or a person you want to network with, find something you can complement honestly (don't ask a question), quickly go into your hook, give the business card(s), thank the client or business affiliate with a firm statement of intention.

Nail Tech: (1) "Oh, I love your necklace, you have a good eye for style. (2) Hi I'm Stella, a local nail-CARE tech in the area, I specialize in relaxing pedicures for tired aching feet. I would love to get those feet in my hot, sudsy water and away those troubles down the drain. (3) Here are two business cards for you or someone you know that need my service. (4) I would love to see you soon, give me a call to schedule your appointment this week.

Cosmetologist: (1) That's a great blouse for a beautiful day. (2) Hi my name is Mary, a local Professional Hair Stylist in the area, I specialize in good old fashioned hair-care. My reputation is built on your recommendation. (3) Here are two business cards for you or someone you know that need my service. (4) I would love to see you soon, give me a call to schedule your appointment this week.

Massage Therapist: (1) I love, love, love those shoes perfect color for spring. (2) Hi my name is Karen, I'm a local Deep Tissue Massage Expert in the area, I specialize in working out the kinks of stress in your body and while at it your body becomes detoxed as well. (3) Here are two business cards for you or someone you know that need my service. (4) I would love to see you soon, give me a call to schedule your appointment this week.

Think of networking, especially if you are an independent BSP. If you are a Stylist, you should have a make-up artist you can partner with. The Make-up artist can come to your salon and make-up your clients face on her wedding day. Think of the time you'd save your client. The make-up artist in return can give your business cards out to their clients. When approaching the potential partner use your hook and peak their interest. The hook is such a professional way to open the door to great results.

✋ Developing your Hook

What are you great at within your profession? _____

_____

What do fantasize about doing more of if you had a choice?_____

_____

What activity do you have so much fun doing, that you'd do it for free? _____

_____

Now, write it in a sentence: _____

_____

Think of a catchy slogan or phrase that flows easily or even rhymes:

_____

_____

_____

_____

Think of other professions that would make a great partnership with you: _____

_____

_____

Set a goal to give 10 business cards a week. That's just 5 people if you give 2 cards at a time. Think of places that are local or central to the BSE where you work. Places you can give cards: Grocery Store Shopper or Cashier, Bank Teller, People at the local nail salon, Gas Station, Childs school teacher, principal, secretary. The list goes on and on for local places with people who need your service.

Thoughts and ideas: _____

_____

_____

_____

_____

_____

_____

_____

Why & How to Market and Advertise for New Clients

In the new age of rapidly changing and evolving technology, computers, telemarketers and information at our finger tips, are you using any of these tools to get new clients or keep in contact with your existing clients? Companies are spending large amounts of cash, time and resources to get names and personal information for potential clients. They are tracking what goods and services *your* clients want. They are using the information they gather to sell goods and services to your clients. **Why** aren't you doing the same?

If you are a longtime Facebook user, you've noticed how much information FB is gathering about you. Back in the good ole' days there were no to very few advertisements for the free FB Service. Now, FB wants to know where you work, shop and eat. Where you went to elementary, Jr. High, high school and college. The tracking companies have a goal to help businesses like Wal-Mart, Target, Macy's, Goodyear, popular catalogs, QVC and HSN give their customers exactly what they want, when they want it. They want this customer that they are tracking to be loyal to them.

As a BSP at the top of your game you are in good shape if you've developed a loyal, faithful following of clients. Most clients, once they find a great BSP are generally very loyal. However you can't take it for granted because the client can be lured away when a loyal friend brags about that new place around the corner that they've found. Oh, it's clean, state of the art equipment, great prices, and friendly service. Your client has only to try that new place once and wonder why they have been loyal to you for so long. On the other hand when a new client sits in your chair, it should become a goal to keep that client and encourage them to bring everyone they know to your BSE-Beauty Service Establishment.

To further convince you that you need to market and advertise your business, today when you get home, check the mailbox for all the post cards and advertisements encouraging you to come in for ½ off. "Buy 1 get one free" offers. "Take 10 % off" offers. How many loyalty plastic tags are hanging on your key chain? Open your personal email and try to find what's important amongst the spam of junk mail offers. Where is your presence, what have you offered your loyal clients and how can your advertisement stand out from the pack?

Salon Affairs is in partnership with the BSP-Beauty Service Professional. We are offering basic Service Success Tools which are designed to help the BSP establish a level of communication and appreciation with their clients. You will use these tools to help gather all the information from your clients so that you can supply their needs and demands. You don't want to risk loosing clients to other BSP's willing to supply and meet your client's demands. OK? OK! With Salon Affairs, your existing clients being fully satisfied will be loyal and become walking advertisement for your services. Existing clients are FREE advertisement. The new clients will be happy they found someone willing to listen and treat them like the valued clients they are with our Service Success Tools.

✍ Take note: It is more cost effective to keep the clients you have, ask them to refer new clients then it will be to spend money on advertising to reach new clients.

The following tools are essential in establishing a professional relationship with your clients. **Service** truly is the foundation of our success. These tools help you provide excellent professional customer service. You get to bond with your client in a whole new professional way. In our test marketing of these tools in our hair salon new clients have stated, "I've never had to fill anything out at the salon." "Wow, I've never had anyone to analyze my hair or give me advice." One excited client exclaimed that she had never had this type of service in the 30 years of getting her hair done. "No one has ever called me by name and informed me of the treatment I was receiving to correct a problem with my hair." Trust and believe, our favorite comment has been, "I will be back, let me make my next appointment."

Clients often stop what they're doing and call when they get the "We've missed you" post card. If any client hasn't called within one week of our sending the cards, we follow up with a phone call to hear, "I was just going to call you, but I've just been so busy." We had one client who called to say, "You didn't have to send me this card thanking me for my co-worker's referral. You did everyone at work a favor by fixing that head." However, I could tell she really did appreciate the thank you card.

No one wants to be taken for granted. Do you want to be taken for granted? **Just remember clients always have options**. Even in the smallest 1 salon towns to the larger metropolitan Beauty Service Establishments on every corner and kitchen. Give your clients the royal, stress free, professional treatment. Thank them, *hook* them give them extra business cards and ask them for referrals. Give them the unexpected. Wow your clients every once in a while. Give your 5, 10, 15 and 20 year anniversary clients something special. Give the kind of treatment you desire.

Thoughts/Ideas: _____

_____

_____

_____

_____

_____

_____

_____

_____

_____

_____

_____

_____

_____

_____

_____

_____

_____

_____

_____

_____

_____

_____

_____

_____

_____

_____

_____

_____

_____

_____

_____

_____

Business Branding

If you don't have one, get a logo. Stat! A logo speaks volumes even when your business may be silent. A logo and a slogan seals your commitment to being a professional. Use your logo and slogan consistently for your business cards, capes, robes and all advertisements. Simply choose a logo from "duty free" websites. You can also pay to have a logo designed exclusively for you. Choose a color within the logo and use it to tie in with the décor of your Business Establishment color scheme. Tie your image all in neatly and make it professional.

What color is the Coca-Cola logo? What animal represents Aflac? Can you sing the State Farm Jingle, and quote lines from their commercial? We ask those questions to help you realize the value of a logo, people remember you and can find you easily. You make your business unforgettable with logos, color and slogans. That's how you "Brand" your business.

Once you have your logo, the entire business color scheme can be tied into it. Emails, websites, business cards, signage should all be consistent with that logo. Your clients will spot it from a distance and associate it with the image you create. They'll easily recognize it and it will distinguish you from your competition. That is important in beginning to establish client loyalty.

In the previous chapter we focused on helping you design your hook. A hook is a crucial part of your business branding. Have you ever spotted a business card that drew you in and made you want to read it. There was a business card once that stated boldly, "The Hair Doctor." The caption read, "We are where to come when your hair is sick." "Free Consultations." My hair was healthy and I remember feeling intrigued by that business card with the little Hair RX logo. I wanted to get a professional consultation from "The Hair Doctor." I once spotted a beautiful logo with swirling orange, blonde and red hair from curling around the top of the business card, it read "The Color Specialist." The mesmerizing beauty of it caught my eye. "We specialize in healthy, bright and beautiful hair color," the slogan read. "Color-corrective Service Available." It made me wonder if I was getting the most out of my color. On impulse I wanted to go see the Hair Doctor and Color Specialist.

Who are you and what service do you specialize in? Highlight it, study it and become the best at it. Then slap a logo, a catch phrase and you're on your way to the big league. Just make sure you **deliver on your promises.**

Am I right about this next sentence? There is nothing worse than being excited about a new offer or promise and then being let down realizing you aren't getting what you were promised. In the business card example above, can you imagine getting to the "Hair Doctor," excited about what you will be told about your hair? You've been thinking about it and waiting on your consultation prescription. Only to have an assistant call you back, shampoo your hair with no consultation. You don't even meet the "Hair Doctor" until it's time to style your hair.

Salon Affairs is not suggesting in any way, shape or form that, the hook, your slogan, your specialty should be a gimmick. A cheap trick to lure clients into your BSE. Give your business branding serious consideration and thought before establishing it and be fully prepared to meet the statement you make with a professional standard of excellence.

Free or Low Cost Marketing to get New Clients

The key to success with the following suggestions, are to know who and where your clients are. Then simply be willing to go and get them, reach out and HOOK them before your competition does. Use your Logo, your Business Brand to make clients remember you. Most of the following ideas can be designed and executed by you, in the comfort of your home office. The cost associated with these low cost Marketing ideas is that you will be doing most of the work and deciding how effective the results are. These ideas can become more expensive when you hire a qualified professional and outsource the work.

Salon Affairs suggests hiring qualified professionals and believes it's worth the investment. Consult your tax preparer because advertising for business is generally tax deductible. When choosing professionals, get 3 quotes for the work and check the Better Business Bureau to make sure the company doesn't have a reputation for disappointing their customers. When you see other logos, business cards or websites that you like, simply inquire to the owner to find out who did the work.

If your advertising budget is slim and or you are not computer savvy, perhaps a relative, friend or even one of your clients has proven to be talented at creating flyers, postcards or helping design logo's. There may be a local print shop nearby you can partner with to keep costs down. If you choose to create advertising on your own, make sure it is free of grammar and spelling errors, spaced properly and appealing. It shouldn't look home-made even if it is. If you're not comfortable with those options hiring a professional to give you that professional image is always the very best option. You'll be so glad you did when you achieve the desired results

1. **Existing Clients:** (a) Ask existing clients for referrals and thank them with an incentive when the new client makes an appointment and keeps it. Make sure all your satisfied clients carry extra business cards with your correct and current information. Please, NO handwritten, scratched out frayed business cards or marketing materials should ever go out to clients. Always remember to thank the client for the referral. (b) Send your existing clients an email flyer with a catchy eye popping promotion, ask that they simply forward to all their address book. The flyer could have a funny picture, joke or coupon to encourage your existing clients to send the email to their friends, family, associates etc. Make this practice every other month or seasonal. Don't become a source of junk mail in your clients email. (c) Give frequent referral cards that you punch, or sign when clients refer new clients. When existing clients successfully refer 5 or 10 clients they get a free service, ½ off or a $25.00 Visa Gift Card, you decide. Make it worth their while then celebrate them on your professional FB page to other clients in the spirit of friendly competition.

2. **Website/Webpage**: (a) Having a web presence keeps your clients informed about the services you offer. You can change services, add services, inform about new services quickly and easily through your webpage. (b) Existing clients can lead friends and family, your potential new clients to your website. (c) New clients using search engines to find local businesses in their area can find you. (d) You can use the web

presence to educate and answer frequently asked questions, celebrate the milestones in the lives of your clients, sell retail and highlight your partners. It's limitless what you can do with a web presence. Trust and believe, you can have a free or low cost webpage much easier than you think. Some Cable carriers offer a free webpage with their business service. Simply Google the words free website and you are more than halfway there. The issue here is, are your clients on the internet. Don't take it for granted, many people do not go on the internet for more than email. There is still a huge population of people who are intimidated and just don't go on the internet. More importantly, speaking of clients that don't go on the internet, are you tech savvy and on the internet because you will need to update your webpage/site to keep it interesting, relevant and beneficial. If you are not tech savvy a single webpage might be your best option. You can post your hours, a short bio, directions, local conveniences and your clients can gain information about your service. If you are more tech savvy, your website could offer client's options like printing coupons, monthly news they can use, they can be made aware of incentives. A one webpage setup is an awesome tool and much simpler than a full website that could be more expensive. A full website may be interactive, accept payments, allow clients to post pictures or fill out forms etc. Consider the advantages and disadvantages and the level of commitment you are willing to make to the venture. It's easy to get over zealous and then realize you've bitten off more than you can chew. Be realistic and willing to ask for help or partner with co-workers to pull it off successfully.

3. **Social Media**: A Facebook Page, Twitter Account, Instagram and LinkedIn are among the more popular of the vast social media market available now. (a) If you decide to take advantage of these free and awesome tools, Salon Affairs

suggests that you make a professional page just for clients, keep your professional and personal pages separate. Use the Pro-page to market your business, inform clients, advertise and inspire them. (b)Using your CCIS, make note of your clients who use the social medium. Please be mindful, take note and **beware** these are public sites. It is just as easy to complain as it is to compliment on these sites. Update and monitor the pages often. If you don't plan to update and monitor the site, its better that you don't start an account. To be successful, change and update pictures, make great positive uplifting comments only. You can suggest new products, give special incentives and do so much on these Social media pages. The key is to visit the site at least once a day and respond timely to questions and comments. You don't have to stop servicing a client to answer, but definitely respond to questions and specific comments within 12 to 24 hours.

4. **<u>Mail or Personally Deliver Advertisements</u>**. (a) While you are out running errands and looking your best, don't be afraid or apprehensive about passing out your business cards. Especially when you are close to your Business Establishment. You'll need to practice in front a mirror or you AP that branding "Hook" to feel comfortable doing this on a regular bases. A "Hook" is a line (script) you throw out to catch your fish (client), such as: *"Hi, I'm* _____. *I specialize in creating updated looks for spring. If you or a friend or two need a new fresh look give me a call. Here are 2 business cards"* (b) Mail or personally deliver flyers, post cards or business cards to local area establishments. Ask that your business card or the flyer be placed on the bulletin board or in the monthly newsletter. Include an incentive such as 1st 5 people to call with the name of the establishment get 10% off. Create flyers that speak to the establishment. For example, if it's a gym or the YMCA the flyer could state "After you sweat the pounds off, let us

sweat the detail of what to do with your hair. Check back frequently with the establishment to make sure you place a fresh flyer or replace the business cards. Local establishments are: Church's, Senior Independent Living Facility, Gym's, YMCA, Recreation Centers, Schools (teachers). You want to make sure the community knows you are there to service their needs locally.

5. **Partner with local businesses**. The same information above, get ready to visit, mail or deliver advertisements to partner with a local business. Being in partnership with a local business simply means that you each offer a mutual or compatible service that could benefit each of your clients. For example, think of becoming a partner with a local barber shop across the way. Perhaps mom could get her hair done while son is getting his hair cut. The Barber should have your advertisement and you should have theirs. If you are a nail tech, partner with a local podiatrist. Hairstylist and Spas should always offer services to Cancer patient Doctors. The locally owned Pizza place next door could place your business card on the back of the menu for all the hungry clients you send their way. They could deliver a free large pizza on Fridays for happy hour or come over and take Saturday morning breakfast orders for the convenience of your clients. You decide the details, meet with the owner and put the partnership in place. Follow up often if you mail items. Set a trial period or time limit on the partnership to make sure it's a good fit and that it is mutually beneficial.

6. **Make your presence known in the community**. The same information above, get ready to mail or deliver advertisements designed specific to the type of local community business or municipality. Being in partnership or making your presence known within the local community simply means that

you make sure people know about your business and the services offer. The local town hall, mayor's office, recreation centers, Laundromat's, leave no stone unturned. Advertise in the community newsletters. Search out the local HOA-Home Owners Associations for local condo's and townhome communities. Advertise in their newsletters or webpages. To be successful, highlight location convenience, special services you offer and offer an incentive. Start by asking your local clients if they have an HOA and ask that they bring a copy of the newsletter. Many community mentor programs, foster care and or adoption agencies need service for their clients. The services you offer don't have to be free. They could be reduced price and scheduled during your slower off peak times such as a Tuesday. Remember that local Church's always get request for people in need. Partner with them for reduced service. The key to this partnership is that you can gain a tax deduction for the reduced or free service and members of the church and their friends may start to patronize your service at full price.

7. **Ask for Clients from Businesses you frequent**. Make sure to let the businesses that you frequent know that you too are in business and seeking clients. If your image is pulled together, you'll feel more comfortable asking for clients. Ask to be linked on their website or if you can place some business cards in the lobby. If those places don't have a community bulletin board, suggest one at your drycleaners, your doctor's office, daycare and your specialty stores. Please don't forget your multi-level marketing reps such as Avon, Tracy Lynn Jewelry and Mary Kay representative. They could become great partnerships. Ask the multi-level reps to put your business card in their goody bag. Not to mention those looking for part-time jobs, sign up with a Multi-level company and sell to your clients. Talk about a perfect fit.

8. **Bulk Mail Advertisement**: Have you ever received a thick envelop full of shiny one page advertisements for several stores in the mail? Valpak comes to mind in Maryland. I've used the coupons and so have other members of my family. The blue envelope will contain advertisements for everything from Pizza Shops to Tire Companies. Well known national branded stores to unknown local mom and pop shops. The companies that distribute this type of bulk mail generally send thousands of those envelopes to various targeted zip codes. That's when knowing your customer comes in handy. If you've collected home address data from your clients, you'll be smarter in your decision to target popular zip codes that you currently service, or other zip codes to get new clients. Partner with other stylist in the Salon or suggest it to the Owner(s).

9. **Buy Advertising in popular magazines**, newspaper, trade publications, depending on your clients. Take a survey or take note of the reading material your clients are reading when they come into your business establishment. When you need a service, where do you look for qualified pros?

10. **Purchase a billboard**, it's not as expensive as you might guess and if you split the cost with a business partner it may be cost effective. A great "Hook" could capture the attention of local traffic and drive business right to your door. Creative advertisement options exist all around you. Even on the local movie screen. The key to this type of advertising is finding out if your client demographic go to the movies. Also you'll need to know which movie theater your client demographic patronize and if they get there early enough to see the advertisement.

Advertising and Marketing is not an exact science. As a business professional try it and then consider if the effort is effective in the end result which is to bring in new clients. Create a way to track what's working. Remember once you get those new clients you want to keep them and have them refer more. **Delivering on your promise is the best form of self-advertising**. Try the suggestions listed above and stick with what works best for you.

TRY! Please don't say you've "tried it all" if you truly have not given these suggestions your best effort. Passing out 10 business cards from a box of 250 is not your best effort. Try out that local Print Shop, they sometimes offer layout options and can create logos. They may want camera ready advertisement, but you won't know if you don't stop in. If you have a professional create a camera ready ad, you may have it copied at Staples, Office Depot, The UPS Store and Kinkos if it's convenient. These Stores offer email copies. That means you can email them your camera ready proof and pick it up at your convenience.

Creative advertisement options exists all around you. If an advertisement has caught your eye, duplicate it without plagiarizing. Be very creative and think of meeting a need. Search the internet and don't be afraid to call and inquire about prices. You'd be surprised at how affordable the options may be.

Thoughts/Ideas: _____

_____

_____

_____

_____

_____

_____

_____

_____

Creating Your Professional Tool Box for Customer Service $uccess

Tool Box for Service Success

If you need to build a house you pick up your tool box, get out the hammer and start to nail. Well … here we go, it's time to build your business and this guide booklet is one of the first tools you'll need to get started. Here are some other tools you need to keep you motivated, inspired and reaching out to touch the heart of your clients.

Setting up your Professional Portfolio

As part of your personal success toolbox there should be a professional Portfolio created to celebrate and honor your career. It will be your motivation to continue learning, achieving, growing and stretching yourself. Inside this Portfolio should be a Resume or Curriculum Vitae listing all of your relevant education, college degrees, trade show attendance, continuing education credits, classes, honors, awards and certificates. Include copies of your certificates, if the originals are hanging in your home office. There should be a current professional headshot of you. Include your professional licenses and other relevant certifications. There should be professional shots of your clients. (Ask clients when celebrating Milestones to take close headshots for your portfolio). It's easier now than ever to take awesome headshots of your clients and print them out from your phone or digital camera at Walmart or the local drugstore kiosk. Also create a brief ½ page bio as well as a full page bio for opportunities that come available for speaking engagements or newspaper articles about you.

Make the Portfolio available for clients to view. Mentoring opportunities and expanding your Beauty Service Professional Career are other reasons to keep an up to date Professional Portfolio.

Thoughts/Ideas: _____

_____

_____

_____

_____

_____

_____

_____

_____

_____

_____

_____

_____

_____

_____

_____

_____

_____

Setting up your Personal Success Journal

A PSJ-Personal Success Journal is your tangible personal motivation for improving within your profession and life in general. It is nothing more than a big fat notebook of inspiration, nothing too fancy or as fancy as you want it. This Guide booklet should be kept in your PSJ along with any and everything that inspires you. Staying motivated, excited and inspired helps to keep you professional. It helps OUR profession. It is so irritating to hear general unfavorable comments about the entire beauty service profession when there are so many great BSP's out in the world.

While attending an EMS-Educational Motivational Symposium at Dudley Products North Carolina, Mr. Joe Dudley once stated at the end of the Symposium that he knew we were excited about what we'd learned. He knew we were pumped up and couldn't wait to get home and try out the new products, skills and tools we were leaving with. He reminded us however that, "motivation is like a slow leak in a tire, you've got to keep airing it up to ride on it." That was a statement most people in the room could relate to because there was a whole lot of head shaking and agreement going on when he made that statement. Just think to yourself right now, have you ever had a slow leaking tire? You have to air it up every couple of days until you get it patched or purchase a new tire. It's a common occurrence and a frequent hazard the more our cities grow. That describes motivation, you have to keep infusing your spirit with words, belief, people, places and actions that inspire you. That's also why we stress developing great habits like the 10 Keys to keeping clientele. Great habits are worth their weight in CASH! Great habits pay dividends to your Professional life! Unlike motivation great habits keep on giving. Motivation takes, takes, takes time and energy but it's worth the effort to encourage yourself to develop great habits.

While shopping, there was a wall hanging that stated in black and white, "A Bad Attitude is like a flat tire, you can't go anywhere until you fix it. Again that tire reference sparked my renewed commitment to stay motivated. I bought that sign and hung it on my wall leading to the basement. I get many comments on it.

A Success Journal can include copies of the really special and meaningful items in your Professional Portfolio as well as articles, poems, thank you notes and things that inspire you. Include blank paper to write or jot down ideas, dreams and goals. By all means the Success Journal should include your copy of this guide booklet. Include business cards from colleagues you meet at trade shows. Include your business partnerships, contracts, Salon Rules and Regulations. The Success Journal should include items important to your success.

Thoughts and Ideas: _____

_____
_____
_____
_____
_____
_____
_____
_____
_____
_____
_____
_____
_____
_____
_____
_____
_____
_____
_____
_____
_____

Your Salon Affairs Marketing Tools for Service Success
Tool
Box

Client Information

1. Client Information, Consultation and Analysis Chart-CCA's ....
   CC1111
2. Address Change Labels for CICA Charts ....
   CC1121
3. Extra Service Sheets for the CCA Charts ....
   CC1131
4. Client Survey/Salon Evaluation Forms ....
   CC1141

Marketing

5. Idea's for brochures, newsletters, special offers and promotions ...
   MK2211
6. Gift Certificates ....
   MK2221
7. Coupon and Special Promotion Cards ....
   MK2231
8. Salon Assistants Handbook ....
   SA3311

Basic Post Cards

1. 'We've missed you' Note Card with reply card ....
   PCMU4411
2. 'Thank you for the referral' & 'Welcome to the Salon' Post Card
   set ... PCTW4421
3. 'Thank you for your loyalty' Post Card ....
   PCTW4431
4. Happy Occasion Set ....
   PCHO4441
   'Happy Birthday', 'Happy Wedding Anniversary',
   'Congratulations', Thanks

5. Support Occasion Set ....
   PCSO4451
   'Get Well', 'Condolence', 'Praying for you' Card Set

6. Sample Package of all Post Cards listed above ....
   PCSA4461

How to use the Marketing Tools for Service Success

1. **Client Information, Consultation and Analysis Chart.**
   The essential and basic CICA Chart. These heavy weight cards 8 ½ x 5 ½ are designed to be placed in an alphabetic index card box or 3 ring binder. Just in case the computer crashes or if you are not technologically savvy yet. Also you can use the cards to input information into your laptop or tablet database. You may be using Quick-Books or a Software system designed for the BSE and just need the manual cards to gather and keep that important information you gather from the clients. By all means keep this information secure. Lock it up in your supply cabinet.

2. **Address Change Labels for CICA Charts.**
   These are simply labels for the CICA Charts that can be placed over the previous address once clients notify you that they have changed their address, email, phone no., etc.

3. **Extra Service Sheets for the CICA Charts**
   On the back of the CICA Chart is a series of lines and dates for you to update your clients services. Making note of hair color, chemical treatment dates and any adverse reactions or allergies the client may have experienced. You will eventually run out of lines. These are the extra sheets to be stapled to the existing CICA cards.

4. **Client Survey/Salon Evaluation Forms**

These 8 ½ x 5 ½ forms are for clients to provide confidential comments and complaints. They come with a quick guide for handling complaints. We suggest purchasing a suggestions box or making one with a lock and a slit for placing the forms easily and confidentially by clients.

5. **Idea's for brochures, newsletters, special offers and promotions**

A brochure outlining ideas for Hooks and other marketing, trade promotions.

6. **Gift Certificates**

A general package of generic gift certificates for Service.

7. **Coupon and Special Promotion Cards**

Business card sized generic coupons and frequent referral cards.

8. **Beauty Service Professional Assistant Handbook**

A booklet for one of the most important jobs in the salon. Often overlooked, the Salon Assistant is either helping to keep clients or running them away. A well trained assistant gives important support to the BSP, helps to maintain the cleanliness and order of the BSE. A poorly trained Assistant is the BSP worst nightmare when left undisciplined, uninspired or not guided to be an asset.

Basic Post Card Sets

The Post cards are non-ethnic general post cards meant to be quickly signed, addressed and mailed. There is room for a quick note if you desire. The topics are self-explanatory and you can request a sample pack that includes each post card.

Sample of Information in the Salon Assistant Handbook

Priority 1: Customer Service
Information on respecting and treating all the BSE clients with kindness and gratitude.
-How to greet clients.
-When to ask for help in dealing with clients.
-How to answer questions and handle client complaints.

Priority 2: Assisting Staff with Trade Responsibilities
-Clearly define Assistants responsibilities to each Staff Member.
-Thoroughly training Assistants & testing their skill & work ethic.
-Training Assistants in Trade Product knowledge as well as Retail Product knowledge.

Priority 3: Maintaining Cleanliness & Order in the BSE-Beauty Service Establishment
-Reviewing all areas of the BSE that will need to be cleaned consistently or periodically.
-Reviewing all expectations of order that will need to be restored in the BSE.
-Reviewing retail area and trade supply areas that will need to be restocked and cleaned.

Priority 4: Job Description
-Informing the Salon Assistant of the chain of command in the salon.
-Helping the Salon Assistant understand their rights in the salon.
-Giving the Salon Assistant the complete and thorough review of their job description

Sample of The Salon Assistant Checklist

1. Always greet clients with a smile.
2. Do not speak loudly to someone else over a client who is being serviced.
3. Do not ask clients personal information.
4. Use your inside professional voice at all times.
5. Ask the Staff Member you are assisting for special instruction for each client.
6. Let the Staff know immediately if there is a problem or concern.
7. Refer the client to Staff to handle complaints.
8. Check the waiting room for cleanliness & order often throughout the day.
9. Check the bathrooms for cleanliness, supplies and order throughout the day.
10. Ensure the floor stays clear of trip hazards and disposable supplies.
11. Clean and sterilize trade supplies.
12. Clean and merchandise retail area.
13. Restock retail area as needed.
14. When in doubt, ask for instruction.
15. 15 Minutes prior to leaving for the day report to staff on your day's progress.

The Last Words & Conclusion

"How to GET and KEEP your clientele"

It is our most sincere desire that reading this guide booklet has opened your mind and heart to the thought of success. Give yourself the gift of success. Please! Be the Hero or Shero in your very own life. You will inspire yourself, your children, your clients and the Beauty Service Industry because you'll be giving the industry a good reputation. Listen to your self-talk, are you talking yourself out of success or preparing for a successful future? I hope your self-talk is not negative and destructive to your spirit, making false statements that suggest you've tried everything and nothing works. In your heart you know that you haven't given any solution your best effort. I pray your self-talk sounds like, "I deserve to reap a harvest of blessings from my honest belief and faith." Or, "My best effort always results in rewards and success that equal more than I could have ever imagined"

Once you **GET** new clients by your successful effort, you must make an effort to turn them into satisfied clients. **Keep** your clients by turning those "10 Keys to Keeping Your Clients" into reality. The 10 Keys are simply good habits. If you perform those habits regularly you will be able to keep your clients coming back. It has worked for me and given me a full, healthy, happy clientele for over 50 years. I can honestly say that I have all the clients I can handle, but at the ripe young age of 70+ years, I'm still getting new clients by referral often. I love this profession. I love this industry and I hate the thought of it being ruined by the bad habits of a few BSUP–Beauty Service UN-Professionals. I can honestly say I still love to go to work and enjoy my clients and my fellow stylists. It's been a joy to stand or sit behind that black chair and give my clients hairstyles for work, vacations, birthday's, weddings, anniversaries and many other happy occasions. Stella and I wish you nothing but an awesome, unstoppable future! Have a great career BSP!

Author Bios

Mary Carver Goldring

The word "Humanitarian," meaning caring, charitable and public spirited are adjectives that accurately and humbly describe Mary Carver-Goldring.

By all whose lives she has touched, Mary Carver Goldring is a joy filled woman with a loving heart of giving back throughout her community in small ways that hugely matter. In every facet of her life she seeks opportunities to bless and encourage those lives that touch hers.

Born the eldest of her five siblings, she was raised in Lexington Tennessee at a time and place when children were expected to help their parents and their fellow man, to be good Christians, gracious and respectful to all. She was born and bred to be a humanitarian. Her extended family, friends, coworkers, church family have known her to be nothing short of the woman she was raised to be.

Mary became a young wife and mother of five children. Fate would step in and the family home would be burned to the ground. With the insurance settlement Mary went to beauty school, opened Mary's Beauty Salon and never looked back. With a heart for people, Mary's Beauty Salon became a place to bring the needs of the community together. Food and Clothing exchanges, collections for displaced families or battered women in need could find help there. It was like Facebook in the 60's making catching up on the latest news and information easy.

As a widowed single mother of five children Mary's cosmetology career was a means of providing security for her young family when she decided to move them from Tennessee to P.G. County Maryland to provide more opportunities for advancement. Her cosmetology career afforded flexibility and the healthy clientele she developed with that southern hospitality allowed her to parent her children keeping them active in their individual interest with all five achieving a high school diploma, as well as sending two children to college. Her eldest daughter followed in her footsteps becoming a cosmetologist and salon owner.

While in Maryland, Mary advanced to Senior Cosmetologist and Salon Owner once again. She has been awarded numerous trophies, plaques and certificates for her technical skill and longevity. Most recently she was awarded the Community Spirit Award from The Training Source Inc. for giving free hair care to women in the welfare to work programs as well as for encouraging her clients to hire some of the women and men in the program. Mary has received recognition throughout the community in various ceremonies, which always surprise and make her wonder, why me. To which all that know her reply you deserve it.

Mary is president of the usher board and a faithful member of Zion Wesley UM Church. She has been a lay speaker as well as served on many other ministries thorough her membership.

Contributing to her very successful 50 year career longevity as a licensed full time Senior Cosmetologist and former Salon Owner, Mary credits frequently attending trade shows and taking continuing education classes especially at Dudley University in Kernersville

North Carolina and Pivot Point in Chicago. As a Dudley Diamond she endorses the Dudley EMS for the education content and value of all trade shows attended. Lastly and just as important if not more so, being genuinely concerned and respectful of her clients time, requests and their needs contributed to building and keeping a very dependable, reliable and devoted clientele base.

Putting this guide booklet together has been a labor of love. I'm so eager to share all that I've learned in this awesome service industry

Stella Carver

It's not who you are that holds you back,
it's who you think you're not.
~Attributed to Hanoch McCarty

Stella has always been a self-motivated leader even in her youth. When Stella's Mother decided to move the family to Prince Georges County Maryland in 1973, it was a fearless opportunity that God had prepared the family for. Even with the merciless teasing about her southern accent, Stella found courage joining various school clubs always staying active and volunteering in her mother's hair salon to learn the family business.

It was in High School that Stella co-founded the Unique Experience Modeling Club and began sponsoring fashion show luncheons almost every weekend in PG County Maryland. This became a huge fund raising event for many local Church's and the word quickly spread. This led to her decision to major in Human Ecology Fashion Merchandising with a minor in Business Administration at The University of Maryland Eastern Shore-UMES.

Stella began her career working in Retail Management. A career that taught her that you don't have a successful business unless you have excellent customer service. The excitement and team leadership were a 20 year challenge of learning and growing in knowledge and skill. It was then that her family businesses grew and they sought Stella's experience. Stella began managing her sister's Dental Office; The Family Smile Shop, her mother's and Sisters Hair Salons; The Family Affair Style Shop I and II. This was a huge full circle experience and brought lasting memories and fun working with her mother and two sisters. While there Stella became a Board Certified Licensed Nail Technician.

Working to bring to life this How to Guide Booklet with her mother, Mary Carver-Goldring has been a dream come true. Sharing the lessons they both have learned in their respective careers has been so exciting and fulfilling. Growing up in a successful family owned "Beauty Shop" was a real experience in Service. It wasn't until years later that Stella would learn from friends and co-workers the terrible experiences and bad habits of some of her fellow BSP's. She was horrified and so unaware that it was as bad as she was being told because her Mother and Sister's Salons were always pleasant, professional places for clients and staff.

Stella has been a motivational speaker, teaching Spiritual Gifts, Self-Esteem, Goal Setting, Female Etiquette and so many other classes at women's retreats, youth workshops and more. Stella knows and teachers that FEAR-False Evidence Appearing Real is often the culprit for missing out on setting and reaching goals. She also believes and has experienced that ALL change for the better begins with a real honest look at the man in the mirror and asking him to change his ways.

Printed in the United States
By Bookmasters